PITMAN SHORTERHAND DICTIONARY

GEORGE A. REID
Chairman, Business Education Department
The Faculty of Education, University of Toronto

Edited by MARION ANGUS
Business Education Consultant
Pitman Publishing

Nov. 78

4.25

NWCC Bookstore

782659

Pitman Publishing
A Division of Copp Clark Limited
Vancouver Calgary Toronto Montreal

ISBN 0 273 042297

PITMAN PUBLISHING
517 Wellington Street West, Toronto, Canada M5V 1G1

COPP CLARK PUBLISHING
517 Wellington Street West, Toronto, Canada M5V 1G1

SIR ISAAC PITMAN AND SONS LTD.
Pitman House, 39 Parker Street, Kingsway, London, W.C.2
P.O. Box 6038, Portal Street, Nairobi, Kenya

SIR ISAAC PITMAN (AUST.) PTY. LTD.
Pitman House, Bouverie Street, Carlton, Victoria 3053, Australia

PITMAN PUBLISHING COMPANY S.A. LTD.
P.O. Box 9898, Johannesburg, S. Africa

PITMAN PUBLISHING CORPORATION
6 Davis Drive, Belmont, California 94002, U.S.A.

Printed and bound in Canada

PREFACE

This *Pitman Shorterhand Dictionary* has been prepared to meet the immediate needs of students, teachers and writers of Pitman Shorterhand for a work of reference that will provide the correct shorthand outlines for most of the frequently used words in the language.

This dictionary is a selected list of words and is not intended in any way to be comprehensive since only the words themselves and their shorthand outlines are given. The Publisher's purpose has been to produce a representative and, in the main, non-technical list of English words that are in common use, or that are likely to be used in dictation across a wide variety of activities in business, industry, the professions and authorship. Inevitably the choice of words for inclusion will not cover all requirements within the bounds of a volume containing between 16 000 and 17 000 entries, but it is hoped that the selection made will satisfy most day-to-day needs.

The list of place names includes all countries in the world and their capitals, and all the larger cities in major countries, especially those in Australasia, Canada, the United States and the British Isles. Many adjectives of nationality are also included.

All the pacers and most of the derivatives in Pitman Shorterhand are shown italicized in the main list and as a complete alphabetical list on page 233. A list of common metric units and their derivatives is included.

The list of proper names is highly selective and is restricted to those most commonly in use.

In order to include as many different words and outlines as possible, repetition has been avoided. For example, a proper name that is also a common word will usually appear in the main list only, and where a town name occurs in more than one country it is included in the list of place names once only. Many surnames are also common words and therefore are to be found in the main list.

Most plurals, present participles and past tenses, unless irregular, are excluded, since the shorthand outlines for these are formed on the regular pattern of circle S, the dot -ing, or the disjoined T or D, but the reader should remember that in some cases a derivative exists where, say, a present tense would rarely if ever be used. In these cases, the derivative is given. However, because shorthand outlines for comparatives, superlatives and adverbs differ, most adjectives are included with their derivatives.

Most homonyms and words with the same spelling but different meanings and pronunciations are included.

Shaded vowel signs appear in this dictionary to conform with the international version of Pitman Shorterhand, entitled Pitman 2000. Slight differences in vowel shading will not be significant to North American students of Shorterhand who do not use this principle, but will meet the needs of international Shorterhand writers.

The writer of Pitman Shorterhand will find it possible to write the shorthand outline for every word in the English language simply by following the rules of the system. It is our belief that as a result of using the *Pitman Shorterhand Dictionary,* all writers of Pitman Shorterhand will increase their basic vocabularies, will read more fluently from printed shorthand, and consequently will write their shorthand outlines with greater speed and confidence.

CONTENTS

A

a	abnormal	absence /
abandon	abnormally	absense absent
abate	aboard	absentee /
abattoir	abode	absolute /
abbey	abolish	absolutely
abbreviate	abolition	absolve
abbreviation	abominable	absorb /
abdicate	aboriginal	absorbent
abdomen	abortive	absorption
abdominal	abound	abstain
abduct	about	abstainer
abduction	abrasion	abstention
abeyance	abrasive	abstinence
abhor	abreast	abstract
abhorrence	abridge	abstraction
abhorrent	abroad	abstruse /
abide	abrogate	absurd
ability	abrogation	absurdity /
ablaze	abrupt	absurdly
able	abruptly	abundance /
able-bodied	abruptness	abundant
ablution	abscess	abundantly
ably	abscond	abuse

abusive	acclaim	accuracy
abusively	acclamation	accurate
abysmal	acclimatize	accurately
abyss	accommodate	accusation
academic	accommodation	accusative
academy	accompani-ment	accuse
accede	accompanist	accustom
accelerate	accompany	ace
acceleration	accomplice	acetylene
accelerator	accomplish	ache
accent	accomplishment	achieve
accentuate	accord	achievement
accentuation	accordance	acid
accept	according	acidity
acceptable	accordingly or	acknowledge
acceptance	accost	acknowledge-ment
access	account	acorn
accessibility	accountable	acoustics
accessible	accountancy	acquaint
accession	accountant	acquaintance
accessory	accrue	acquiesce
accident	accumulate	acquiescence
accidental	accumulation	acquire
accidentally	accumulator	acquisition

2

acquisitive	acutely	adherent
acquit	adage	adhesion
acquittal	adamant	adhesive
acre	adapt	adieu
acreage	adaptability	adjacent
acrid	adaptable	adjective
acrimonious	adaptation	adjoin
acrimoniously	adapter	adjourn
across	add	adjournment
acrylic	adder	adjudicate
act	addict	adjust
action	addiction	adjustment
actionable	addition	adjutant
activate	additional	administer
active	additionally	administrate
actively	additive	administration
activity	address	administrative
actor	addressee	adminis-tratively
actress	adept	administrator
actual	adequacy	admirable
actually	adequate	admiral
actuary	adequately	Admiralty
acumen	adhere	admiration
acute	adherence	admire

3

admirer		advancement		advocacy
admissible		advantage		advocate
admission		advantageous		aerial
admit		advantageously		aerodrome
admittance		advantages		aerodynamics
admittedly		adventitious		aeronautic
admonish		adventure		aeroplane
adolescence		adventurer		aerosol
adolescent		adventuress		aerospace
adopt		adverb		aesthetic
adoption		adversary		affability
adorable		adverse		affable
adoration		adversely		affably
adore		adversity		affair
adorn		advertise		affect
adornment		advertisement		affectation
adrenalin		advertiser		affection
adrift		advice		affectionate
adroit		advisability		affectionately
adsorb		advisable		affidavit
adulation		advise		affiliate
adult		advisedly		affiliation
adultery		adviser		affinity
advance		advisory		affirm

4

affirmative		aggravate		aground			
affix		aggravation		ah			
afflict		aggregate		ahead			
affliction		aggregation		aid			
affluence		aggression		ail			
afford		aggressive		ailment			
affront		aggressively		aim			
afloat		aggressor		aimless			
aforesaid		aggrieve		aimlessly			
afraid		aghast		air			
afresh		agile		airborne			
after		agility		aircraft			
aftermath		agitate		airfield			
afternoon		agitation		airily			
afterthought		agitator		airline			
afterwards		agnostic		airmail			
again		ago		airman			
against		agonizing		airway			
age		agony		airworthy			
ageless		agree		aisle			
agency		agreeable		ajar			
agenda		agreement		akin			
agent		agricultural		alabaster			
aggrandizement		agriculture		alacrity			

5

alarm		allay		*almost*		
alas		allegation		alms		
albeit		allege		alone		
albumen		allegiance		along		
alcohol		allegory		alongside		
alcoholic		allergic		aloof		
alcove		alleviate		aloud		
alderman		alley		alphabet		
ale		alliance		aphabetical		
alert		allocate		alphabetically		
alertness		allocation		alpine		
alfalfa		allot		already		
alias		allotment		*also*		
alibi		allow		altar		
alien		allowable		alter		
alienate		allowance		alteration		
alienation		alloy		alternate, *v*		
alight		allude		alternate, *adj*		
align aline		allure		alternately		
alignment alinement		alluringly		alternative		
alike		ally		alternatively		
alimony		almighty		although		
alive		almond		altitude		
all		almoner		*altogether*		

6

altruistic	ambush	amphibious
aluminium	ameliorate	ample
aluminum	amen	amplification
always	amenable	amplifier
am	amend	amplify
amalgamate	amendment	amply
amalgamation	amenity	amputate
amass	amiable	amputation
amateur	amiably	amuse
amaze	amicable	amusement
amazement	amicably	*an*
amazingly	amid	anachronism
ambassador	amidst	anaemia / anemia
amber	amiss	anaemic / anemic
ambidexterous	ammunition	anaesthetic / anesthetic
ambient	amnesty	anagram
ambiguity	among	analogous
ambiguous	amongst	analogy
ambiguously	amoral	analyse / analyze
ambition	amorous	analysis
ambitious	amorously	analyst
ambitiously	amorphous	analytic
amble	amount	analytical
ambulance	ampersand	analytically

anarchist

anarchy

anathema

anatomical

anatomy

ancestor

ancestral

anchor

anchorage

anchovy

ancient

and

anecdote

anemometer

anew

angel

anger

angle

angler

Anglican

anglicize

Anglo-Saxon

angrily

angry

anguish

angular

angularity

animal

animate

animation

animosity

animus

aniseed

ankle

annals

annexation

annexe
annex

annihilate

annihilation

anniversary

annotate

annotation

announce

announcement

announcer

annoy

annoyance

annual

annually

annuity

annul

annum

anoint

anomalous

anomaly

anonymity

anonymous

anonymously

another

answer

answerable

ant

antagonism

antagonist

antagonistic

antagonize

antecedent

antedate

anthem

anthology

anthrax

anthropology

8

antibiotic	anyhow	appeal	
antic	anyone	appear	
anticipate	*anything*	appearance	*or*
anticipation	anyway	appease	
anticlimax	anywhere	append	
anticlockwise	apart	appendage	
anticyclone	apartment	appendices	
antidote	apathetic	appendicitis	
antipathy	apathy	appendix	
antipodes	ape	appendixes	
antiquarian	aperture	appertain	
antiquated	apex	appetite	
antique	apiece	appetize	
antiquity	apologetic	applaud	
antiseptic	apologize	applause	
antisocial	apology	apple	
antithesis	apostle	appliance	
antler	apostrophe	applicable	
anvil	appal	applicant	
anxiety	apparatus	application	
anxious	apparel	apply	
anxiously	apparent	appoint	
any	apparently	appointment	
anybody	apparition	apportion	

9

apposite	approximate	archaic
appraisal	approximately	archbishop
appraise	approximation	archery
appreciable	April	archipelago
appreciably	apron	architect
appreciate	apropos	architectural
appreciation	apt	architecture
appreciative	aptitude	archives
apprehend	aptly	ardent
apprehension	aptness	ardently
apprehensive	aquarium	ardour ardor
appre- hensively	aquatic	arduous
apprentice	aqueduct	*are*
apprenticeship	arable	area
apprise	arbiter	arena
approach	arbitrarily	argue
approachable	arbitrary	argument
approbation	arbitrate	argumenta- tive
appropriate	arbitration	arid
appropriately	arbitrator	aridity
appropriation	arc	arise
approval	arcade	arisen
approve	arch	aristocracy
approvingly	archaeology	aristocrat

10

aristocratic	arrogance	asbestos
arithmetic	arrogant	ascend
ark	arrogantly	ascendancy
		ascendency
arm	arrow	ascent
armament	arsenal	ascertain
armature	arsenic	ascribe
armchair	arson	ash
armistice	art	ashamed
armour	arterial	ashore
armor		
armoury	artery	aside
army	artful	ask
aroma	artfully	askance
aromatic	arthritis	askew
arose	article	asleep
around	articulate	aspect
arouse	artificial	asphalt
arraign	artificially	asphyxia
arrange	artillery	aspirant
arrangement	artisan	aspirate, *n*
array	artist	aspirate, *v*
arrear	artistic	aspiration
arrest	artistically	aspire
arrival	artless	ass
arrive	*as*	assail

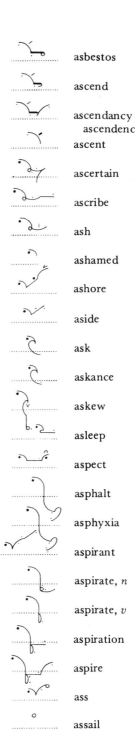

11

assailant	assistant	astutely
assassin	assizes	asunder
assassinate	associate	asylum
assault	association	at
assay	assort	ate
assemble	assortment	atheism
assembly	assume	athlete
assent	assumption	athletic
assert	assurance	atlas
assertion	assure	atmosphere
assess	assuredly	atmospheric
assessment	asterisk	atom
assessor	asthma	atomic
asset	astonish	atone
assiduously	astonishment	atonement
assign	astound	atrocious
assignation	astray	atrociously
assignee	astride	atrocity
assignment	astringent	attach
assignor	astrologer	attachment
assimilate	astronaut	attack
assimilation	astronomer	attain
assist	astronomy	attainable
assistance	astute	attainment

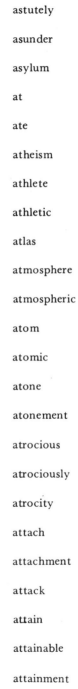

12

attempt		audaciously		author	
attend		audacity		authoress	
attendance		audibility		authoritative	
attendant		audible		authoritatively	
attention		audibly		authority	
attentive		audience		authorization	
attentively		audio-typist		authorize	
attest		audio-visual		authorship	
attestation		audit		auto	
attester attestor attic		audition		autobiography	
attire		auditor		autocracy	
attitude		auditorium		autocrat	
attorney		aught		autocratic	
attract		augment		autograph	
attraction		August		automatic	
attractive		aunt		automatically	
attractively		auspices		automation	
attributable		auspicious		automobile	
attribute		auspiciously		autonomy	
auburn		austere		autopsy	
auction		austerity		autumn	
auctioneer		authentic		auxiliary	
audacious		authenticate		avail	
		authenticity		availability	

13

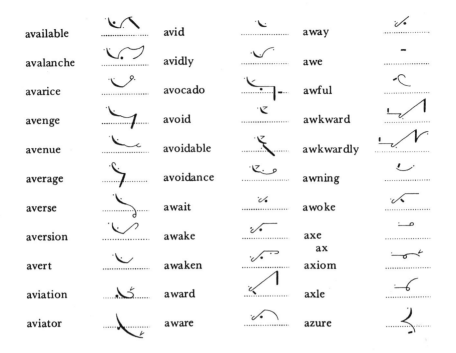

available	avid	away
avalanche	avidly	awe
avarice	avocado	awful
avenge	avoid	awkward
avenue	avoidable	awkwardly
average	avoidance	awning
averse	await	awoke
aversion	awake	axe
		ax
avert	awaken	axiom
aviation	award	axle
aviator	aware	azure

B

baby	bake	banana
babyish	baker	band
bachelor	bakery	bandage
back	balance	bandit
backbencher	balance-sheet	bandstand
background	balcony	bandwagon
backhanded	bald	bandy
backlash	balderdash	bane
backlog	baldly	bang
backwards	bale	banish
bacon	ball	banishment
bacteria	ballad	banister
bad	ballast	bank
bade	ballet	banker
badge	ballistics	bankrupt
badly	balloon	bankruptcy
baffle	ballot	banner
bag	balm	banns
baggage	balmy	banquet
bail	balsam	baptism
bailey	bamboo	baptize
bailiff	ban	bar
bait	banal	barbarian

15

barber

barbican

barbiturate

bard

bare

barefaced

barely

bargain

barge

bark

barley

barn

barometer

barometric

baron

baroness

barrack

barrage

barrel

barren

barrenness

barricade

barrier

barrow

barter

base

baseball

baseboard

baseless

basement

bash

bashful

bashfully

basic

basically

basin

basis

bask

basket

basketball

baste

bastion

bat

batch

bath

bathe

bather

bathroom

baton

battalion

batten

batter

battery

battle

battle-axe

battlefield

battleship

bauxite

bawl

bay

bayonet

bazaar

be

beach

beacon

bead

beak

beam

bean

bear

bearable

beard

bearer		bedstead	begin
beast		bedtime	beginner
beastly		bee	begrudge
beat		beech	beguile
beaten		beef	begun
beau		beehive	behalf
beautician		beeline	behave
beautiful		been	behaviour behavior
beautifully		beer	behead
beautify		beeswax	beheld
beauty		beet	behind
beaver		beetle	behold
became		beetroot	beholder
because		befall	behoove
beckon		befallen	beige
become		befell	being
bed		befit	belated
bedcover		before	belfry
bedding		beforehand	belief
bedeck		befriend	believable
bedouin		beg	believe
bedridden		began	believer
bedrock		beget	belittle
bedroom		beggar	bell

17

belligerent	benighted	betray
bellow	benign	betrayal
belly	benignant	betroth
belong	benignly	betrothal
belovèd	bent	better
below	bequeath	betterment
belt	bequest	between
bemoan	berate	betwixt
bench	bereave	beverage
bend	bereavement	bevy
beneath	bereft	beware
benediction	beret	bewilder
benefactor	berry	bewilderment
benefactress	berth	bewitch
benefice	beseech	beyond
beneficence	beset	biannual
beneficent	beside	bias
beneficial	besiege	bib
beneficially	besmirch	Bible
beneficiary	besought	biblical
benefit	best	bibliography
benevolence	bestial	biceps
benevolent	bestow	bicker
benevolently	bet	bicycle

18

bid	binoculars	bivouac
bidder	biographer	bizarre
biennial	biographical	black
big	biography	blackberry
bigamist	biological	blackbird
bigamy	biology	blackboard
bigger	bipartisan	blacken
biggest	birch	blackguard
bigot	bird	blackmail
bigotry	birth	blacksmith
bigwig	birthday	bladder
bile	birthmark	blade
bilge	birthplace	blame
bilingual	birthright	blameless
bilious	biscuit	blameworthy
biliousness	bisect	bland
bill	bishop	blandly
billet	bit	blank
billiards	bite	blanket
billion	bitten	blankly
billow	bitter	blare
binary	bitterness	blaspheme
bind	bitumen	blast
binder	bituminous	blatant

19

blatantly	blister	blue	
blaze	blithe	bluebell	
bleach	blithely	blueberry	
bleak	blithesome	blue-*eyed*	
bleat	blitz	bluff	
bled	blizzard	blunder	
bleed	bloated	blunt	
bleep	block	bluntly	
blemish	blockade	blur	
blend	blockhead	blurb	
bless	blond	blurt	
blessèd	blonde		
blest	blood	blush	
blew	bloodthirsty	bluster	
blight	bloom	boar	
blind	blossom	board	
blindfold	blot	boarder	
blindly	blotch	boast	
blindness	blotter	boastful	
blink	blotting-paper	boastfulness	
bliss	blouse	boat	
blissful	blow	bob	
blissfully	blown	bobbin	
blissfulness	blubber	bobsleigh	
	bludgeon	bode	

20

bodily		bond		boost	
body		bondage		booster	
boffin		bone		boot	
bog		boneless		booth	
bogey		bonfire		border	
boggle		bonnet		bore	
bogus		bonus		bored	
boil		booby		boredom	
boiler		book		born	
boisterous		bookbinder		borne	
boisterously		bookcase		borough	
bold		bookkeeper		borrow	
bolder		bookkeeping		borrower	
boldest		booklet		bosom	
boldly		bookmaker		boss	
boldness		bookmark		botanist	
bollard		bookseller		botany	
bolster		bookshelf		botch	
bolt		bookstall		both	
bomb		bookstore		bother	
bombard		bookworm		bothersome	
bombastic		boom		bottle	
bomber		boon		bottleneck	
bombshell		boor		bottom	

21

boudoir		boyhood		brave		
bough		boyish		bravely		
bought		boyishly		bravery		
boulder bowlder		brace		brawl		
boulevard		bracelet		brawn		
bounce		bracken		bray		
bound		bracket		brazen		
boundary		brackish		brazenly		
boundless		brag		breach		
bountiful		braid		bread		
bounty		Braille		breadth		
bouquet		brain		breadwinner		
bourgeois		brainless		break		
bout		brainwash		breakable		
bow, n		braise		breakage		
bow, v		brake		breakdown		
bowels		bran		breakfast		
bower		branch		breakwater		
bowl		brand		breast		
bowler		brandish		breath		
box		brandy		breathe		
boxer		brash		breathless		
boy		brass		bred		
boycott		bravado		breech		

22

breed		brighter		broadest	
breeder		brightest		broadly	
breeze		brightly		broadminded	
breezily		brightness		brocade	
breezy		brilliance		brochure	
brethren		brilliancy		brogue	
brevity		brilliant		broil	
brew		brilliantly		broke	
bribe		brim		broken	
bribery		brimful		brokenhearted	
brick		brine		broker	
bricklayer		bring		bromide	
bridal		brink		bronchial	
bride		brinkmanship		bronchitis	
bridegroom		brisk		bronze	
bridge		briskly		brooch	
bridle		bristle		brood	
brief		brittle		broody	
briefcase		broach		brook	
briefly		broad		broom	
brigade		broadcast		broth	
brigand		broadcasting		brother	
bright		broaden		brotherhood	
brighten		broader		brother-*in*-law	

23

brought		buddy		bulletin	
brow		budge		bullet-proof	
browbeat		budget		bullion	
brown		buff		bullock	
browse		buffalo		bull's-*eye*	
bruise		buffer		bully	
brunette		buffet		bulwark	
brunt		buffoon		bump	
brush		bug		bumper	
brushwood		buggy		bumpkin	
brusque		bugle		bumptious	
brusquely		bugler		bumptiousness	
brutal		build		bun	
brutality		builder		bunch	
brutally		building		bundle	
brute		build-up		bung	
bubble		built		bungalow	
buccaneer		bulb		bungle	
buck		bulbous		bunk	
bucket		bulge		bunker	
buckle		bulk		bunting	
buckwheat		bulky		buoy	
bucolic		bull		buoyancy	
bud		bullet		buoyant	

buoyantly		burrow	butler
burble		bursar	butt
burden		burst	butter
burdensome		bury	button
bureau		bus	button-hole
bureaucracy		bush	buttress
burg		bushel	buxom
burgh		bushy	buy
burglar		busier	buyer
burglary		busiest	buzz
burial		busily	buzzer
burlesque		business	by, bye
burly		businesslike	by-election
burn		bust	bygone
burner		bustle	by-law, bye-law
burnish		busy	by-product
burnt		*but*	bystander
burr		butcher	byword

C

cab	calculable	cameo	
cabbage	calculate	camera	
cabin	calculation	cameraman	
cabinet	calculator	camouflage	
cable	caldron	camp	
cablegram	calendar	campaign	
cachet	calf	camphor	
cackle	calibration	campus	
cactus	calibre caliber	can	
cad	calico	canal	
cadence	call	canary	
cadet	caller	cancel	
cadge	callous	cancellation	
cadre	callow	cancer	
café	calm	candid	
cafeteria	calmly	candidacy	
cage	calorie	candidate	
cairn	calumny	candidature	
cajole	cam	candidly	
cake	camber	candle	
calamitous	cambric	candlestick	
calamity	came	candour candor	
calcium	camel	candy	

26

cane		capacity		caravan	
canine		cape		carbide	
canister		capillary		carbine	
canker		capital		carbolic	
cannibal		capitalist		carbon	
cannon		capitalization		carbonic	
cannot		capitalize		carburettor	
canoe		capitation		carcass	
canon		capitulate		card	
canopy		caprice		cardboard	
cant		capricious		cardiac	
can't		capsize		cardigan	
canteen		capsule		cardinal	
canter		captain		cardiogram	
canton		caption		care	
canvas		captivate		career	
canvass		captivation		careful	
canvasser		captive		carefully	
canyon		captivity		careless	
cap		captor		carelessly	
capability		capture		carelessness	
capable		car		caress	
capably		caramel		caret	
capacious		carat		caretaker	

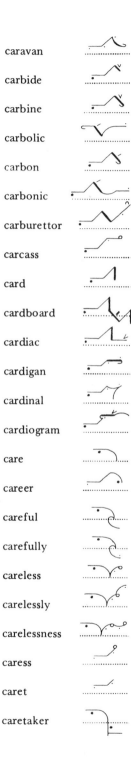

27

careworn		cascade		cataract		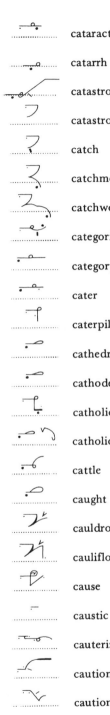
cargo		case		catarrh		
caricature		casework		catastrophe		
caries		cash		catastrophic		
carnival		cashew		catch		
carnivorous		cashier		catchment		
carol		cashmere		catchword		
carouse		casino		categorize		
carpenter		cask		category		
carpentry		casket		cater		
carpet		cassette		caterpillar		
carriage		cast		cathedral		
carrier		caste		cathode		
carrot		castigate		catholic		
carry		cast-iron		catholicism		
cart		castle		cattle		
cartage		castor		caught		
carte blanche		casual		cauldron		
cartel		casualty		cauliflower		
carton		casuistry		cause		
cartoon		cat		caustic		
cartoonist		cataclysm		cauterize		
cartridge		catalogue catalog		caution		
carve		catapult		cautionary		

cautious		cellulose		cereal	
cautiously		Celtic		ceremonial	
cavalcade		cement		ceremonially	
cavalry		cemetery		ceremonious	
cave		censor		ceremony	
cavern		censorship		certain	
cavil		censure		certainly	
cavity		cent		certainty	
cease		centenary		certificate	
ceaseless		centennial		certification	
ceaselessly		centigrade		certify	
cedar		centigram		cessation	
cede		centilitre		cession	
ceiling		centime		cesspit	
celebrate		centimetre		chafe	
celebration		centipede		chaff	
celebrity		central		chagrin	
celery		centralization		chain	
celestial		centralize		chair	
celibacy		centrally		chairman	
celibate		centre center		chairmanship	
cell		centrifugal		chalet	
cellar		century		chalk	
celluloid		ceramics		challenge	

29

challenger	charade	chatter
chamber	charcoal	chauffeur
champagne	charge	chauvinist
champion	chargeable	cheap
championship	chariot	cheapen
chance	charismatic	cheaper
chancel	charitable	cheapest
chancellor	charitably	cheaply
chancery	charity	cheapness
change	charlatan	cheat
changeable	charm	check
changeless	charred	checker
channel	chart	checkout
chant	charter	cheek
chaos	chase	cheep
chaotic	chasm	cheer
chaotically	chassis	cheerful
chap	chaste	cheerfully
chapel	chasten	cheerfulness
chaperon	chastise	cheerless
chaplain	chastisement	cheéry
chapter	chastity	cheese
character	chat	cheeseparing
characteristic	chattel	chef

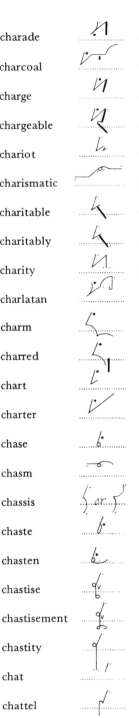
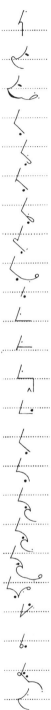

30

chemical		chill		choke	
chemist		chilly		cholera	
chemistry		chime		choose	
cheque		chimney		chop	
cheque-book check-book		chimpanzee		chopper	
cherish		chin		choral	
cherry		china		chord	
cherub		chink		chore	
chess		chip		chorister	
chest		chiropodist		chorus	
chestnut		chirp		chose	
chevron		chisel		chosen	
chew		chit		Christ	
chic		chivalrous		christen	
chicken		chivalry		Christendom	
chide		chloride		Christian	
chief		chlorine		Christianity	
chiefly		chloroform		Christmas	
child		chock		chromatic	
childhood		chocolate		chromium	
childish		choice		chromosome	
childishly		choicer		chronic	
childless		choicest		chronicle	
children		choir		chronological	

chronologically	circular	civilian
chrysalis	circularize	civility
chrysan-themum	circulate	civilization
chubby	circulation	civilize
chuck	circumference	clad
chum	circumlocution	claim
chunk	circumscribe	claimant
church	circumspect	clairvoyance
churchyard	circumspection	clairvoyant
churlish	circumstance	clamber
churlishly	circumstantial	clammy
churn	circumstantially	clamour clamor
chute	circumvent	clamp
cider	circus	clan
cigar	cist	clandestine
cigarette	cistern	clang
cinch	citadel	clap
cinder	citation	claret
cinema	cite	clarification
cinematograph	citizen	clarify
cipher	citizenship	clarion
circle	city	clarionet
circuit	civic	clarity
circuitous	civil	clash

32

clasp	clearing house	climber
class	clearly	clinch
classic	clearness	cling
classical	clear-sighted	clinic
classification	cleave	clinical
classify	cleft	clinically
classmate	clemency	clink
classroom	clench	clinker
clatter	clergy	clip
clause	clergyman	clique
claustrophobia	cleric	cloak
claw	clerical	clock
clay	clerk	clockwork
clean	clerkship	clod
cleaner	clever	clog
cleanest	cliché	cloister
cleanliness	click	close
cleanly	client	closely
cleanse	clientele	closet
cleanser	cliff	close-up
clear	climate	closure
clearance	climatic	clot
clearer	climax	cloth
clearest	climb	clothe

cloud		coarsen		coercion	
clover		coast		coeval	
clown		coaster		coexist	
cloy		coastguard		coffee	
club		coastline		coffer	
clubhouse		coat		cog	
cluck		coax		cogent	
clue		coaxial		cogently	
clump		cobber		cogitate	
clumsily		cobbler		cogitation	
clumsy		cobweb		cognac	
clung		cocaine		cohere	
cluster		cock		coherence	
clutch		cockney		coherent	
clutter		cocktail		cohesion	
coach		cocoa		cohesive	
coagulate		coconut		coiffure	
coal		cocoon		coil	
coalesce		cod		coin	
coal-field		coddle		coinage	
coalition		code		coincide	
coal-mine		codicil		coincidence	
coarse		codify		coke	
coarsely		coerce		cold	

34

colder		colliery		combustion	
coldest		collision		come	
cold-hearted		colloquial		comedian	
coldly		colloquialism		comedy	
coldness		colloquially		comely	
coleslaw		collusion		comet	
colic		colon		comfort	
collaborate		colonel		comfortable	
collaboration		colonial		comfortably	
collaborator		colonist		comforter	
collapse		colony		comic	
collapsible		colossal		comical	
collar		colour color		comically	
collate		colourful		comma	
collateral		colourless		command	
collation		colt		commandeer	
colleague		column		commander	
collect		coma		commemorate	
collection		comb		commemoration	
collective		combat		commence	
collector		combatant		commencement	
college		combination		commend	
collegiate		combine		commendable	
collide		combustible		commendably	

commendation	commonwealth	compatibility
commensurate	commotion	compatible
comment	communicate	compel
commentary	communication	compendium
commerce	communion	compensate
commercial	communism	compensation
commercialize	communist	compete
commercially	community	competence
commiserate	commute	competent
commissar	commuter	competently
commission	compact	competition
commissioner	companion	competitive
commit	companionship	competitively
commitment	company	competitor
committal	comparable	compilation
committee	comparative	compile
commodious	comparatively	compiler
commodity	compare	complacency
common	comparison	complacent
commoner	compartment	complacently
commonest	compass	complain
commonly	compassion	complainant
commonplace	compassionate	complaint
commonsense	compassionately	complement

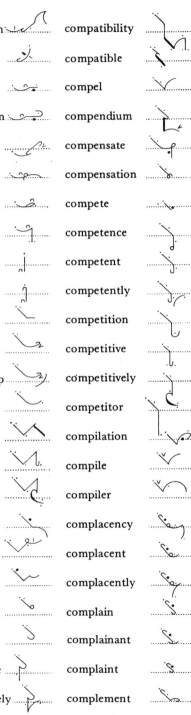
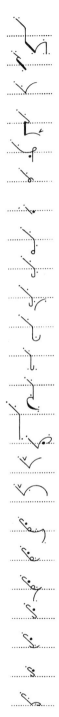

36

complementary	comprehend	conceivably
complete	comprehensible	conceive
completely	comprehension	concentrate
completeness	comprehensive	concentration
completion	compress	concentric
complex	compression	concept
complexion	compressor	conception
complexity	comprise	concern
compliance	compromise	concert
compliant	compulsion	concession
complicate	compulsive	conciliate
complication	compulsively	conciliation
complicity	compulsorily	conciliatory
compliment	compulsory	concise
complimentary	compunction	concisely
comply	computation	conciseness
component	compute	conclude
compose	computer	conclusion
composer	comrade	conclusive
composite	concave	conclusively
composition	conceal	concoct
compositor	concede	concoction
composure	conceit	concord
compound	conceivable	concourse

37

concrete		conductor		conflagration	
concur		conduit		conflict	
concurrence		cone		confluence	
concurrent		confection		conform	
concurrently		confectioner		conformity	
concussion		confectionery		confound	
condemn		confederate		confront	
condemnation		confederation		confuse	
condemnatory		confer		confusion	
condensation		conference		confute	
condense		confess		congeal	
condenser		confession		congenial	
condescend		confidante		congenially	
condescension		confide		congenital	
condign		confidence		congestion	
condiment		confident		conglomeration	
condition		confidential		congratulate	
conditional		confidently		congratulations	
conditionally		confine		congregate	
condole		confinement		congregation	
condolence		confirm		congregational	
condone		confirmation		congress	
conducive		confiscate		congressional	
conduct		confiscation		congressman	

38

conical	consecrate	consignor
conifer	consecration	consist
conjecture	consecutive	consistency
conjugal	consecutively	consistent
conjugate	consensus	consistently
conjunction	consent	consolation
conjunctive	consequence	console
conjuncture	consequent	consolidate
conjure	consequential	consolidation
connect	consequently	consonant
connection connexion	conservation	consonantal
connivance	conservative	consort
connive	conservatively	consortium
connoisseur	conserve	conspectus
connotation	consider	conspicuous
conquer	considerable	conspicuously
conqueror	considerably	conspiracy
conquest	considerate	conspire
conscience	considerately	constable
conscientious	consideration	constant
conscientiously	consign	constantly
conscious	consignee	constellation
consciously	consigner	consternation
consciousness	consignment	constituency

39

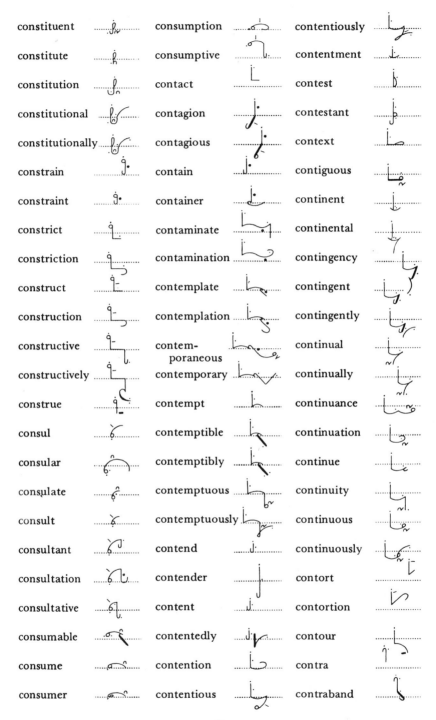

constituent	consumption	contentiously
constitute	consumptive	contentment
constitution	contact	contest
constitutional	contagion	contestant
constitutionally	contagious	context
constrain	contain	contiguous
constraint	container	continent
constrict	contaminate	continental
constriction	contamination	contingency
construct	contemplate	contingent
construction	contemplation	contingently
constructive	contem-poraneous	continual
constructively	contemporary	continually
construe	contempt	continuance
consul	contemptible	continuation
consular	contemptibly	continue
consulate	contemptuous	continuity
consult	contemptuously	continuous
consultant	contend	continuously
consultation	contender	contort
consultative	content	contortion
consumable	contentedly	contour
consume	contention	contra
consumer	contentious	contraband

40

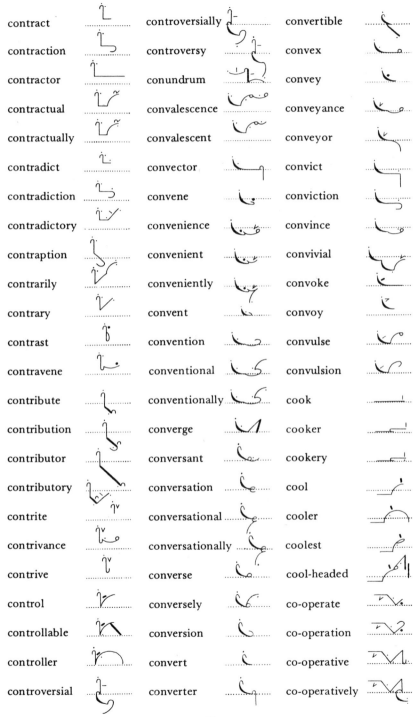

contract	controversially	convertible
contraction	controversy	convex
contractor	conundrum	convey
contractual	convalescence	conveyance
contractually	convalescent	conveyor
contradict	convector	convict
contradiction	convene	conviction
contradictory	convenience	convince
contraption	convenient	convivial
contrarily	conveniently	convoke
contrary	convent	convoy
contrast	convention	convulse
contravene	conventional	convulsion
contribute	conventionally	cook
contribution	converge	cooker
contributor	conversant	cookery
contributory	conversation	cool
contrite	conversational	cooler
contrivance	conversationally	coolest
contrive	converse	cool-headed
control	conversely	co-operate
controllable	conversion	co-operation
controller	convert	co-operative
controversial	converter	co-operatively

41

co-operator		core		correspond	
co-opt		co-respondent		correspondence	
co-ordinate		cork		correspondent	
co-ordination		corkscrew		corridor	
copartnership		corn		corroborate	
cope		corner		corroboration	
copious		corollary		corroborative	
copiously		coronary		corrode	
copper		coroner		corrosion	
copse		corporate		corrosive	
copy		corporation		corrugated	
copy-book		corps		corrupt	
copyhold		corpse		corruption	
copyright		corpulence		cosh	
copy-writer		corpulent		cosmetic	
coquettish		corpus		cosmic	
coral		corral		cosmopolitan	
cord		correct		cost	
cordage		correction		costliness	
cordial		corrective		costly	
cordiality		correctly		costume	
cordially		correctness		cosy	
cordon		correlate		cot	
corduroy		correlation		coterie	

42

cottage	counting-house	cover
cotton	countless	coverage
couch	country	covert
cough	countryman	covet
could	countryside	covetous
council	county	coxswain
councillor councilor	coup	cow
counsel	coupé	coward
counsellor counselor	couple	cowardice
count	coupon	cowardly
countenance	courage	cow-hide
counter	courageous	coy
counteract	courageously	cozily
counter-balance	courier	cozy
counter-blast	course	crab
counter-claim	court	crack
counterfeit	courteous	crackle
counter-feiter	courteously	cradle
counterfoil	courtesy	craft
countermand	court-house	craftily
counterpart	courtroom	craftiness
countersign	courtyard	craftsman
counter-vailing	cousin	crafty
countess	covenant	crag

43

cram	credential	crevice
cramp	credibility	crew
cranberry	credible	crib
crane	credibly	cricket
crank	credit	crime
crash	creditable	criminal
crass	creditably	criminally
crate	creditor	crimson
crater	credulity	cringe
crave	credulous	crinkle
crawl	creed	cripple
crayon	creek	crisis
craze	creep	crisp
crazy	cremate	criterion
creak	creole	critic
cream	creosote	critical
crease	crepe	critically
create	crept	criticism
creation	crescent	criticize criticise
creative	crest	critique
creatively	crestfallen	croak
creator	cretaceous	crochet
creature	cretin	crockery
credence	cretonne	crocodile

croft		crude		cuckoo		
crony		crudity		cucumber		
crook		cruel		cuddle		
crooked		cruelly		cudgel		
crookedly		cruelty		cue		
crop		cruise		cuff		
cropper		cruiser		cuisine		
croquet		crumb		culinary		
cross		crumble		culminate		
cross-breed		crumple		culmination		
cross-examination		crunch		culpable		
cross-examine		crusade		culprit		
crossly		crush		cult		
crossroads		crust		cultivate		
crossword		crutch		cultivation		
crotchet		crux		cultural		
crouch		cry		culturally		
crow		crypt		culture		
crowd		crystal		cumbersome		
crown		crystallize		cumulative		
crucial		cub		cumulatively		
crucifix		cube		cuneiform		
crucifixion		cubic		cunning		
crucify		cubicle		cunningly	or	

45

cup	cursèd	cut	
cupboard	cursive	cute	
curable	cursorily	cutlery	
curate	cursory	cutlet	
curb	curt	cut-out	
cure	curtail	cutter	
curfew	curtailment	cyanide	
curio	curtain	cycle	
curiosity	curtly	cyclical	
curious	curvature	cyclist	
curiously	curve	cyclone	
curl	cushion	cylinder	
curly	custard	cylindrical	
currant	custodian	cynic	
currency	custody	cynical	
current	custom	cynically	
currently	customarily	cynicism	
curricula	customary	cynosure	
curriculum	customer	cypher	
curry	custom-house	cyst	
curse	customs	cytology	

D

dab	danger	dawn
dabble	dangerous	day
Dad	dangerously	daybreak
Daddy	dangle	daylight
daily	dare	daytime
daintily	daringly *or.*	daze
dainty	dark	dazzle
dairy	darken	dead
dais	darker	deaden
daisy	darkest	deadline
dale	darkness	deadlock
dam	darling	deadly
damage	darn	deaf
damask	dart	deafen
dame	dash	deal
damp	dashboard	dealer
dampen	data	dealt
damper	date	dean
dampness	daub	*dear*
damsel	daughter	dearer
dance	daunt	dearest
dancer	dauntless	dearly
dandy	dawdle	dearth

death	deceitfulness	declension
deathly	deceive	decline
débâcle	December	decode
debar	decency	decompose
debase	decent	decomposition
debatable	decently	decontrol
debate	decentralize	decorate
debauch	deception	decoration
debenture	deceptive	decorative
debility	deceptively	decorator
debit	decide	decorous
debonair	decidedly	decorum
débris	deciduous	decoy
debt	decimal	decrease
debtor	decipher	decree
début	decision	decrepit
débutante	decisive	decry
decade	decisively	dedicate
decadence	deck	dedication
decant	declaim	deduce
decay	declarable	deduct
decease	declaration	deduction
deceit	declare	deed
deceitful	declassify	deem

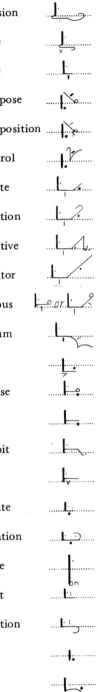

48

deep		defiance		degradation	
deepen		defiant		degrade	
deeper		deficiency		dehydrate	
deepest		deficient		deity	
deeply		deficiently		deject	
deface		deficit		dejection	
defacement		define		delay	
defamation		definite		delectable	
defamatory		definitely		delegate	
defame		definition		delegation	
default		definitive		delete	
defect, v		deflate		deletion	
defect, n		deflation		deliberate, v	
defective		deflect		deliberate, adj	
defence defense		deform		deliberation	
defenceless		deformity		delicacy	
defend		defraud		delicate	
defendant		defray		delicious	
defensible		deft		delight	
defensive		deftly		delightful	
defensively		defunct		delightfully	
defer		defy		delimitation	
deference		degenerate, v		delineate	
deferment		degenerate, adj		delinquency	

49

delinquent	demote	department
delirious	demur	departmental
deliver	demure	departmentally
deliverance	demy	departure
delivery	denial	depend
delude	denier	dependable
deluge	denigrate	dependably
delusion	denim	dependant
demand	denomination	dependence
demarcate	denominational	dependency
demeanour demeanor	denote	dependent
demise	denounce	depict
democracy	dense	deplete
democrat	densely	depletion
democratic	density	deplorable
democratically	dent	deplore
demon	dental	deploy
demonstrable	dentist	deport
demonstrate	dentistry	deportment
demonstration	denture	depose
demonstrative	denude	deposit
demonstratively	denunciation	depository
demonstrator	deny	depot
demoralize	depart	deprave

50

depravity		descend		desk	
deprecate		descendant		desolate	
depreciate		descent		desolation	
depreciation		describe		despair	
depress		description		despatch	
depression		descriptive		desperate	
deprivation		descriptively		desperately	
deprive		desecrate		desperation	
depth		desecration		despicable	
deputation		desegregate		despise	
depute		desert		despite	
deputize		deserter		despondency	
deputy		desertion		despondent	
derelict		deserve		despotic	
dereliction		deservedly		despotism	
deride		design		dessert	
derision		designate		destination	
derisive		designation		destine	
derivation		designer		destiny	
derivative		desirability		destitute	
derive		desirable		destitution	
dermatitis		desire		destroy	
dermatology		desirous		destroyer	
dervish		desist		destruction	

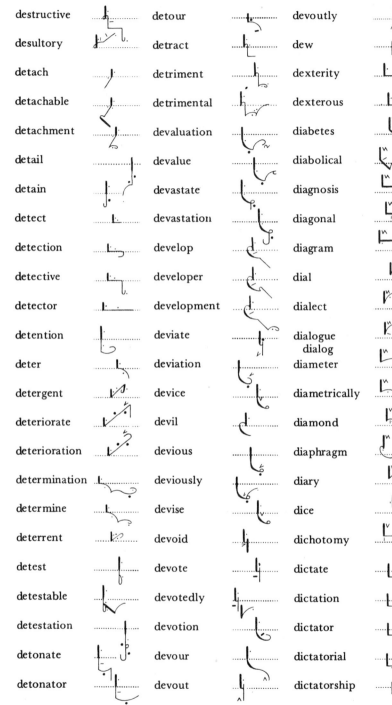

destructive	detour	devoutly
desultory	detract	dew
detach	detriment	dexterity
detachable	detrimental	dexterous
detachment	devaluation	diabetes
detail	devalue	diabolical
detain	devastate	diagnosis
detect	devastation	diagonal
detection	develop	diagram
detective	developer	dial
detector	development	dialect
detention	deviate	dialogue dialog
deter	deviation	diameter
detergent	device	diametrically
deteriorate	devil	diamond
deterioration	devious	diaphragm
determination	deviously	diary
determine	devise	dice
deterrent	devoid	dichotomy
detest	devote	dictate
detestable	devotedly	dictation
detestation	devotion	dictator
detonate	devour	dictatorial
detonator	devout	dictatorship

52

diction	digger	diminutive
dictionary	digit	din
did	dignify	dine
didactic	dignitary	diner
diesel	dignity	dinghy
diet	digress	dingo
dietary	digression	dingy
dieter	dike	dinner
differ	dilapidate	diocese
difference	dilapidation	dip
different	dilate	diphtheria
differential	dilatory	diploma
differentiate	dilemma	diplomacy
differently	dilettante	diplomat
difficult	diligence	diplomatic
difficulty	diligent	diplomatically
diffidence	diligently	dire
diffident	dilute	direct
diffuse	dilution	direction
dig	dim	directive
digest	dime	directly
digestible	dimension	director
digestion	diminish	directorate
digestive	diminution	directory

53

dirge	disavow	discount
dirt	disbelieve	discourage
dirty	disburse	discouragement
disability	disbursement	discourse
disable	disc / disk	discover
disabuse	discard	discovery
disadvantage	discern	discredit
disaffected	discernible	discreditable
disagree	discernment	discreet
disagreeable	discharge	discreetly
disagreement	disciple	discrepancy
disappear	discipline	discretion
disappearance	disclaim	discriminate
disappoint	disclose	discursive
disappointment	disclosure	discus
disapprobation	discolour / discolor	discuss
disapproval	discomfort	discussion
disarm	discommode	disdain
disarmament	disconnect	disease
disarrange	disconsolate	disembark
disarray	discontent	disembarkation
disaster	discontinue	disenchanted
disastrous	discord	disenfranchise
disastrously	discordant	disengage

54

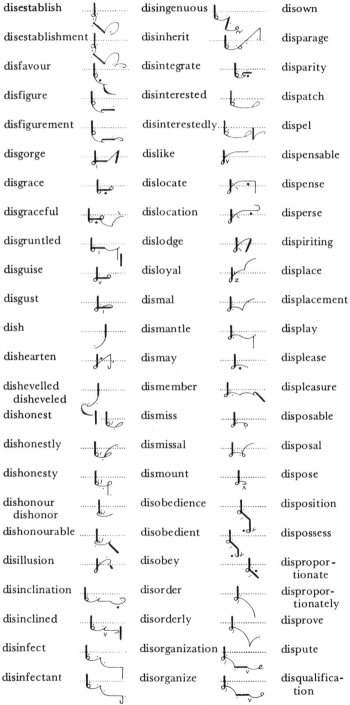
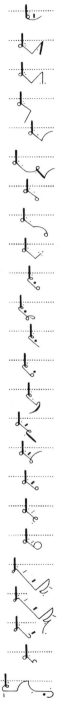

disestablish	disingenuous	disown
disestablishment	disinherit	disparage
disfavour	disintegrate	disparity
disfigure	disinterested	dispatch
disfigurement	disinterestedly	dispel
disgorge	dislike	dispensable
disgrace	dislocate	dispense
disgraceful	dislocation	disperse
disgruntled	dislodge	dispiriting
disguise	disloyal	displace
disgust	dismal	displacement
dish	dismantle	display
dishearten	dismay	displease
dishevelled disheveled	dismember	displeasure
dishonest	dismiss	disposable
dishonestly	dismissal	disposal
dishonesty	dismount	dispose
dishonour dishonor	disobedience	disposition
dishonourable	disobedient	dispossess
disillusion	disobey	dispropor-tionate
disinclination	disorder	dispropor-tionately
disinclined	disorderly	disprove
disinfect	disorganization	dispute
disinfectant	disorganize	disqualifica-tion

55

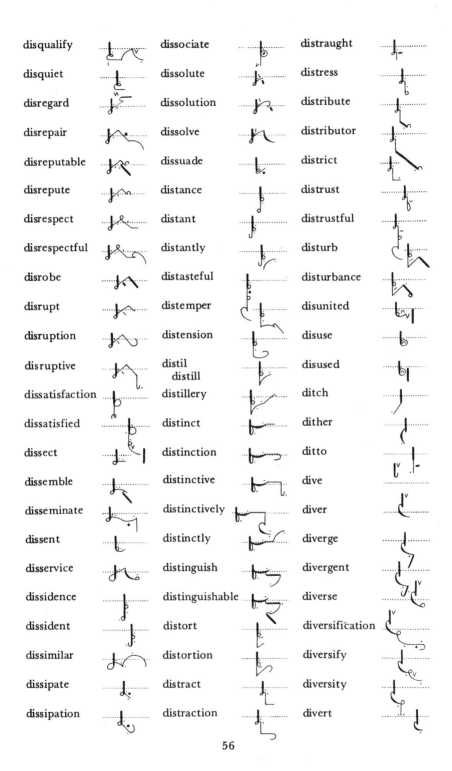

disqualify	dissociate	distraught
disquiet	dissolute	distress
disregard	dissolution	distribute
disrepair	dissolve	distributor
disreputable	dissuade	district
disrepute	distance	distrust
disrespect	distant	distrustful
disrespectful	distantly	disturb
disrobe	distasteful	disturbance
disrupt	distemper	disunited
disruption	distension	disuse
disruptive	distil distill	disused
dissatisfaction	distillery	ditch
dissatisfied	distinct	dither
dissect	distinction	ditto
dissemble	distinctive	dive
disseminate	distinctively	diver
dissent	distinctly	diverge
disservice	distinguish	divergent
dissidence	distinguishable	diverse
dissident	distort	diversification
dissimilar	distortion	diversify
dissipate	distract	diversity
dissipation	distraction	divert

56

divest		documentation		donate	
divide		dodge		donation	
dividend		does		done	
divine		doff		donkey	
divinely		dog		donor	
divinity		dogfight		doom	
divisible		doggerel		door	
division		dogma		doorway	
divisional		dogmatic		dope	
divisive		dole		dormant	
divorce		doleful		dormitory	
divulge		doll		dosage	
dizzily		*dollar*		dose	
dizzy		dolphin		dossier	
do		dolt		dot	
docile		domain		dotage	
docker		dome		double	
docket		domestic		doubly	
dockyard		domicile		doubt	
doctor, Dr.		dominant		doubtful	
doctrinal		dominate		doubtfully	
doctrine		domination		doubtingly	
document		domineer		doubtless	
documentary		dominion		dough	

doughnut	dramatist	drew	
doughty	drank	dried	
dour	drape	drier	
douse	drapery	drift	
dove	drastic	drill	
dowdy	drastically	drily	
down	draught	drink	
downcast	draughty	drinker	
downfall	draw	drip	
downhearted	drawback	drive	
downhill	drawer	drivel	
downpour	drawl	driven	
downright	drawn	driver	
downstairs	dray	drizzle	
downwards	dread	drone	
doze	dreadful	droop	
dozen	dream	drop	
drab	dreamt	drop-out	
dragon	dreary	drought	
drain	dredge	drove	
drainage	drench	drown	
drake	dress	drowsiness	
drama	dresser	drowsy	
dramatically	dressmaker	drudge	

58

drudgery		duel		duration	
drug		duet		duress	
druggist		dug		during	
druid		duke		dusk	
drum		dull		dusky	
drummer		duly		dust	
drunk		dumb		duster	
drunkard		dumbfounded		dutiful	
drunken		dummy		duty	
drunkenness		dump		dwarf	
dry		dun		dwell	
dryer		dunce		dweller	
dual		dune		dwelt	
dubious		dungeon		dwindle	
dubiously		dupe		dye	
duck		duplicate		dyer	
duckling		duplication		dynamic	
duct		duplicator		dynamite	
ductile		duplicity		dynamo	
dud		durability		dynasty	
due		durable		dyspepsia	

E

each	Easter	eddy	
eager	eastern	edge	
eagerly	eastward	edgeways	
eagle	easy	edible	
ear	eat	edict	
earache	eaten	edification	
earl	eaves	edifice	
earlier	ebb	edify	
earliest	ebony	edit	
early	ebullient	edition	
earn	eccentric	editor	
earnest	eccentricity	editorial	
earnestly	ecclesiastic	editorially	
earth	echo	editorship	
earthenware	eclipse	educate	
earthly	economic	education	
earthquake	economical	educational	
ease	economically	educationally	
easel	economist	educator	
easier	economize	Edwardian	
easiest	economy	eerie	
easily	ecstasy	eerily	
	extasy		
east	ecumenical	efface	

effacement	eight *8 or*	electric
effect	eighteen *18 or*	electrically
effective	eighteenth *18(or*	electricity
effectively	eighth *8(or*	electrification
effectiveness	eightieth *80(or*	electrify
effectual	eighty *80.or*	electrode
effeminate	either	electrolysis
effeminately	ejaculate	electronic
effervesce	eject	elegance
efficacious	eke	elegant
efficiency	elaborate, *v*	elegantly
efficient	elaborate, *adj*	element
efficiently	elaborately	elementary
effigy	elaboration	elephant
effluent	elapse	elevate
effort	elastic	elevation
effrontery	elasticity	elevator
effusive	elated	eleven *11 or*
egalitarian	elbow	eleventh *11(or*
egg	elder	elicit
ego	eldest	eligibility
egotistical	elect	eligible
eh	election	eliminate
eider-down	electorate	elimination

61

elite	embarrassment	eminence
Elizabethan	embassy	eminent
ellipsis	embellish	eminently
elocution	embezzle	emissary
elongate	embezzlement	emit
elope	embezzler	emollient
eloquence	embitter	emolument
eloquent	emblem	emotion
eloquently	embody	emperor
else	embolism	emphasis
elsewhere	embrace	emphasize
elucidate	embrocation	emphatic
elude	embroider	emphatically
elusive	embroidery	empire
elusively	embryo	empirical
emaciate	embryonic	empirically
emanate	emendation	employ
emancipate	emerald	employee
emancipation	emerge	employer
embankment	emergency	employment
embargo	emetic	empower
embark	emigrant	empress
embarkation	emigrate	empty
embarrass	emigration	emu

emulate	endless	enhance
emulation	endlessly	enigma
emulsify	endorse	enigmatic
emulsion	endorsement	enigmatically
enable	endow	enjoin
enact	endowment	enjoy
enactment	endurable	enjoyable
enamel	endurance	enjoyment
enamour enamor	endure	*enlarge*
enchant	enemy	*enlargement*
encircle	energetic	*enlarger*
enclose	energetically	enlighten
enclosure	energy	enlightenment
encounter	enervate	enlist
encourage	enfold	enlistment
encouragement	enforce	enliven
encroach	enforcement	enmity
encumber	engage	enormity
encyclopaedia	engagement	enormous
end	engine	enormously
endanger	engineer	enough
endear	engrave	enquire
endeavour endeavor	engraver	enquiry
endemic	engross	enrage

63

enraptured	entirely	epic	
enrich	entirety	epicure	
enrol enroll	entitle	epidemic	
enrolment enrollment	entity	epilepsy	
ensemble	entomology	episcopal	
ensign	entourage	episode	
enslave	entrance	epistle	
ensnare	entrant	epitaph	
ensue	entreaty	epoch	
ensure	entrée	equable	
entail	entrepreneur	equal	
entangle	entrust	equality	
enter	entry	equalization	
enterprise	enumerate	equalize	
entertain	enunciate	equally	
entertainer	enunciation	equation	
entertainment	envelop	equator	
enthral	envelope	equatorial	
enthusiasm	enviable	equilibrium	
enthusiastic	envious	equinox	
enthusiastically	environment	equip	
entice	envoy	equipment	
enticement	envy	equitable	
entire	ephemeral	equitably	

equity		escape		ethical	
equivalent		escort		ethically	
equivocal		eskimo		ethics	
era		esoteric		ethos	
eradicate		especial		etiquette	
erase		especially		euphemism	
erect		espionage		euthanasia	
erection		esquire		evacuate	
erode		essay		evacuation	
erosion		essayist		evade	
erotic		essence		evaluate	
err		essential		evaluation	
errand		establish		evaporate	
errant		establishment		evasion	
erratic		estate		evasive	
erratically		esteem		evasively	
erroneous		estimate		eve	
erroneously		estimation		even	
error		estuary		evening	
erudite		et cetera, etc.		evenly	
erupt		eternal		event	
eruption		eternally		eventful	
escalate		eternity		eventual	
escapade		ethereal		eventuality	

65

eventually	exalt	excise	
ever	examination	excite	
evergreen	examine	excitement	
everlasting	examiner	exclaim	
everlastingly	example	exclamation	
every	exasperate	exclude	
everybody	excavate	exclusion	
everyone	excavation	exclusive	
every*thing*	exceed	exclusively	
everywhere	exceedingly	excommunicate	
evict	excel	excursion	
eviction	excellence	excusable	
evidence	excellent	excuse	
evident	excellently	execute	
evidently	except	execution	
evil	exception	executive	
evocative	exceptional	executor	
evolution	exceptionally	executrix	
evolve	excerpt	exemplary	
exacerbate	excess	exemplify	
exact	excessive	exempt	
exactly	excessively	exemption	
exaggerate	exchange	exercise	
exaggeration	exchequer	exert	

exertion

exhale

exhaust

exhaustion

exhaustive

exhibit

exhibition

exhibitor

exhilarate

exhilaration

exhort

exhortation

exhume

exile

exist

existence

existent

exit

exonerate

exorbitant

exorcism

exotic

exotically

expand

expanse

expansion

expansive

expect

expectant

expectantly

expectation

expediency

expedient

expediently

expedite

expedition

expel

expend

expendable

expenditure

expense

expensive

experience

experiment

experimental

experimen-
tally

expert

expertly

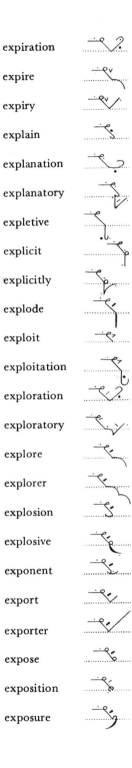

expiration

expire

expiry

explain

explanation

explanatory

expletive

explicit

explicitly

explode

exploit

exploitation

exploration

exploratory

explore

explorer

explosion

explosive

exponent

export

exporter

expose

exposition

exposure

express		externally		extreme	
expression		extinct		extremely	
expressive		extinction		extremity	
expressly		extinguish		extricate	
expropriate		extinguisher		extrovert	
expulsion		extol		exuberance	
exquisite		extortion		exuberantly	
exquisitely		extra		exude	
extemporary		extract		exult	
extend		extraction		eye	
extension		extradite		eyeball	
extensive		extradition		eyebrow	
extensively		extraneous		eyelash	
extent		extraneously		eyelid	
extenuate		extra-ordinarily		eye-opener	
extenuation		extra-ordinary		eyesight	
exterior		extravagance		eyesore	
exterminate		extravagant		eye-strain	
external		extravagantly		eye-witness	

68

F

fable		failure		falter	
fabric		faint		fame	
fabrication		faintly		familiar	
fabulous		fair		familiarity	
façade		fairer		familiarization	
face		fairest		familiarize	
facetious		fairly		family	
facetiously		fairness		famine	
facial		fairy		famish	
facile		faith		famous	
facilitate		faithful		fan	
facility		faithfully		fanatic	
facsimile		faithless		fanatical	
fact		fake		fanaticism	
faction		fall		fanciful	
factor		fallacious		fancy	
factory		fallacy		fantastic	
factual		fallen		fantastically	
factually		false		fantasy	
faculty		falsehood		far	
fade		falsely		farce	
Fahrenheit		falsification		farcical	
fail		falsify		fare	

69

farewell	father	feather	
farm	father-*in*-law	feathery	
farmer	fatherland	feature	
farmhouse	fathom	February	
farmyard	fatigue	fed	
far-reaching	fatten	federal	
farther	faucet	federation	
farthest	fault	fee	
fascinate	faultless	feeble	
fascination	faulty	feed	
fascism	favour favor	feel	
fashion	favourable favorable	feet	
fashionable	favourably favorably	feint	
fashionably	favourite favorite	felicitate	
fast	favouritism favoritism	felicity	
fasten	fear	fell	
fastener	fearful	fellow	
faster	fearfully	fellowship	
fastest	fearless	felon	
fastidious	fearsome	felony	
fatal	feasibility	felt	
fatality	feasible	female	
fatally	feast	feminine	
fate	feat	fence	

70

fend	feud	fierce
fender	feudal	fiercely
fennel	fever	fiercer
ferment	feverish	fiercest
fermentation	feverishly	fiery
fern	few	fifteen
ferocious	fewer	fifteenth
ferociously	fiancé(e)	fifth
ferocity	fiasco	fiftieth
ferry	fiat	fifty
fertile	fibre fiber	fig
fertility	fibreglass	fight
fertilization	fibrositis	fighter
fertilize	fickle	figment
fertilizer	fiction	figurative
fervent	fictitious	figuratively
fervently	fiddle	figure
fervour fervor	fidelity	figure-head
fester	fidget	filament
festival	fidgety	file
festivity	field	filibuster
fetch	fiend	fill
fete	fiendish	filler
fetter	fiendishly	fillet

film		finish		fishhook	
filter		finite		fishy	
filth		fire		fission	
filthy		firearms		fissure	
filtration		fireman		fist	
fin		fireplace		fit	
final		fireproof		fitful	
finale		fireside		fitment	
finality		fireworks		fitness	
finalize		firm		fitter	
finally		firmament		fittest	
finance		firmer		fittingly	
financial		firmest		five	
financially		firmly		fix	
financier		first		fixation	
find		first-aid		fixative	
finder		first-class		fixedly	
fine		first-hand		fixture	
finely		firstly		fizzle	
finer		first-rate		flabbergasted	
finesse		fiscal		flabby	
finest		fish		flaccid	
finger		fisher		flag	
fingerprint		fishery		flagon	

72

flagrant		flax		flit		
flagrantly		flay		float		
flair		flea		flock		
flake		fled		flog		
flamboyant		flee		flood		
flame		fleece		floor		
flange		fleet		flop		
flank		flesh		floral		
flannel		flew		florid		
flannelette		flex		florist		
flap		flexibility		floss		
flapper		flexible		flotation		
flare		flick		flotsam		
flash		flicker		flounce		
flask		flight		flounder		
flat		flimsy		flour		
flatly		flinch		flourish		
flatten		fling		flout		
flatter		flint		flow		
flattery		flip		flower		
flaunt		flippant		flowery		
flavour flavor		flippantly		flown		
flaw		flirt		fluctuate		
flawless		flirtatious		fluctuation		

73

flue		focus	
fluency		fodder	
fluent		foe	
fluently		fog	
fluffy		foggy	
fluid		foil	
fluke		foist	
flung		fold	
fluorescent		folder	
fluoride		foliage	
flurry		folio	
flush		folk	
fluster		folklore	
flute		follow	
flutter		follower	
flux		folly	
fly		fond	
flyer flier		fondle	
flyover		fondly	
flyweight		food	
flywheel		fool	
foal		foolhardy	
foam		foolish	
fob		foolishly	
focus		foolproof	
fodder		foolscap	
foe		foot	
fog		football	
foggy		footboard	
foil		foothold	
foist		footmark	
fold		footnote	
folder		footpath	
foliage		footprint	
folio		footstep	
folk		footwear	
folklore		for	
follow		forage	
follower		foray	
folly		forbade forbad	
fond		forbear	
fondle		forbearance	
fondly		forbid	
food		forbidden	
fool		force	
foolhardy		forceful	
foolish		forcefully	
foolishly		forceps	

74

forces	forestry	format	formation
forcibly	foretell	formative	former
ford	forever	formerly	formidable
fore	forewarn	formula	formulate
foreboding	foreword	forsake	fort
forecast	forfeit	forth	forthcoming
foreclose	forfeiture	forthright	forthwith
foreclosure	forge	fortieth	fortify
forego	forger	fortitude	fortnight
foregone	forgery	fortress	fortuitous
forehead	forget	fortunate	fortunately
foreign	forgetful	fortune	forty
foreigner	forgive		
foreman	forgiveness		
foremost	forgo		
forensic	forgot		
forerunner	forgotten		
foresee	fork		
foreseen	forlorn		
foreshadow	forlornly		
foreshore	form		
foreshorten	formal		
forest	formality		
forestall	formally		

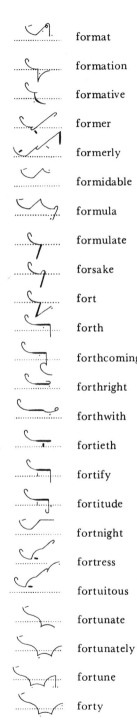
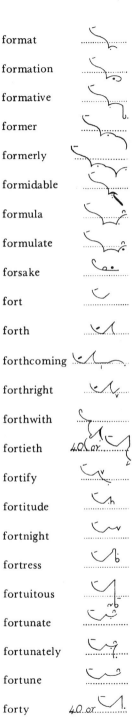

forum		fracture		fray	
forward		fragile		freak	
fossil		fragment		free	
foster		fragmentary		freedom	
fought		fragrance		freehold	
foul		fragrant		freelance	
foully		frail		freely	
found		frailty		freer	
foundation		frame		freest	
founder		framer		freewill	
foundry		franc		freeze	
fount		franchise		freight	
fountain		frank		freighter	
four		frankly		frenzy	
foursome		frankness		frequency	
four-square		frantic		frequent	
fourteen		frantically		frequently	
fourteenth		fraternal		fresh	
fourth		fraternally		freshen	
fowl		fraternity		fresher	
fox		fraud		freshest	
fracas		fraudulent		freshly	
fraction		fraudulently		fret	
fractious		fraught		fretful	

76

fretwork	frock	fruition
friar	frog	fruitless
friction	frolic	fruitlessly
Friday	from	frump
fried	front	frustrate
friend	frontage	frustration
friendless	frontal	fry
friendliness	frontier	fudge
friendly	frontispiece	fuel
friendship	frost	fugitive
frieze	frostbite	fulfil fulfill
frigate	frosty	fulfilment fulfillment
fright	froth	full
frighten	frown	full-length
frightful	froze	fullness fulness
frightfully	frozen	full-stop
frigid	frugal	fully
frill	frugality	fulminate
fringe	frugally	fumble
frisk	fruit	fume
fritter	fruiterer	fumigate
frivolity	fruitful	fun
frivolous	fruitfully	function
fro	fruitfulness	functional

functionary	furl	furthest	
fund	furlong	furtive	
fundamentally	furlough	furtively	
fund-raising	furnace	fury	
funeral	furnish	fuse	
funereal	furnisher	fusion	
fungus	furniture	fuss	
funnel	furore	fussy	
funnier	furrier	futile	
funniest	furrow	futility	
funny	further	future	
fur	furtherance	futurist	
furious	furthermore	futuristic	
furiously	furthermost	fuzzy	

78

G

gable	galore	garish
gadget	galosh / golosh	garland
Gaelic	galvanize	garment
gag	gambit	garnish
gaiety	gamble	garret
gaily	gambol	garrison
gain	game	garrulous
gainful	gammon	garter
gainfully	gamut	gas
gainsay	gang	gas-cooker
gait	gangrene	gash
gala	gangster	gasket
galaxy	gangway	gasoline / gasolene
gale	gaol	gasp
gall '	gap	gas-stove
gallant	gape	gastric
gallantly	garage	gate
gallantry	garb	gate-house
gallery	garbage	gatepost
galley	garbled	gather
gallon	garden	gauche
gallop	gardener	gaudy
gallows	gargle	gauge / gage

79

gaunt	generously	geometry
gauntlet	genesis	geriatrics
gauze	genetics	germ
gave	genial	germinate
gavotte	geniality	gestation
gay	genially	gesticulate
gaze	genius	gesture
gazette	genteel	get
gear	Gentile	geyser	or
geese	gentility	ghastly
gelatine	gentle	ghost
gem	gentleman	ghoulish
gender	gentlemanly	giant
genealogy	gentlemen	gibe
general	gentleness	giddy
generality	gently	gift
generalization	genuine	gigantic
generalize	genuinely	gild
generally	geographical	gill (of a fish)
generate	geographically	gill (a measure)
generation	geography	gilt
generator	geological	gilt-edged
generosity	geologist	gimmick
generous	geology	gin

ginger		gland		glorify	
gingerly		glandular		glorious	
gipsy / gypsy		glare		gloriously	
gird		glass		glory	
girder		glassful		gloss	
girdle		glassware		glossary	
girl		glassy		glossier	
girlish		glaze		glossiest	
girlishly		gleam		glossy	
giro		glean		glove	
girth		glee		glow	
gist		glib		glucose	
give		glibly		glue	
given		glide		glum	
glacier		glimmer		glumly	
glad		glimpse		glut	
gladden		glint		glutinous	
glade		glitter		glutton	
gladly		gloaming		gluttonous	
gladness		gloat		gluttonously	
glamorous		globe		glycerin(e)	
glamorously		gloom		gnarled	
glamour		gloomily		gnash	
glance		gloomy		gnaw	

go		gooseberry		grade	
goad		gorge		gradient	
go-ahead		gorgeous		gradual	
goal		gorgeously		gradually	
goat		gorgonzola		graduate	
go-between		gospel		graduation	
goblet		gossip		graft	
God		got		grain	
godly		gouge		grammar	
goes		gourmet		grammatical	
gold		gout		grammatically	
golden		govern		gramme	
golf		government		granary	
gone		govern-mental		grand	
gong		governor		grandchild	
good		governorship		grand-daughter	
good-bye		gown		grandeur	
good-humoured		grab		grandfather	
good-looking		grace		grandmother	
good-natured		graceful		grandparent	
goodness		gracefully		grandson	
good-night		gracious		granite	
goodwill		graciously		grant	
goose		gradation		grantor	

granular		gravitation		grieve	
granulate		gravity		grievous	
grape		gravy		grievously	
graph		graze		grill grille	
graphic		grease		grim	
graphically		greasy		grimace	
graphite		great		grime	
grapple		greater		grimly	
grasp		greatest		grin	
grass		greatly		grind	
grassy		greatness		grip	
grate		greed		gripe	
grateful		greedily		grisly	
gratefully		greedy		grist	
gratification		green		gristle	
gratify		greengrocer		grit	
gratis		greenhouse		groan	
gratitude		greet		grocer	
gratuity		gregarious		grocery	
grave		grenade		groom	
gravedigger		grew		groove	
gravel		grey gray		grope	
gravely		grief		gross	
graven		grievance		grotesque	

83

ground	guarantee	gull
groundless	guarantor	gullet
groundwork	guard	gullible
group	guardian	gulp
grove	guess	gum
grovel	guesswork	gumption
grow	guest	gun
grower	guesthouse	gunfire
growl	guidance	gunpowder
grown	guide	gurgle
growth	guideline	gush
grub	guild	gust
grudge	guilder	gusto
grudgingly	guile	gut
gruelling	guilt	gutter
gruesome	guiltily	guy
gruff	guilty	guzzle
gruffly	guise	gymnasium
grumble	guitar	gymnastics
grumpy	gulden	gyrate
grunt	gulf	gyroscope

H

habilitate	hallow	hand-out	
habit	Halloween	handsome	
habitation	halo	handsomely	
habitual	halt	handwork	
habitually	halter	handwriting	
hack	halve	handy	
hackle	ham	hang	
hackneyed	hamlet	hangar	
had	hammer	hanger	
haddock	hammock	hanker	
haemorrhage hemorrhage	hamper	haphazard	
hag	hamstrung	hapless	
haggard	hand	happen	
haggis	handbag	happier	
haggle	handbook	happiest	
hail	handcuff	happiness	
hair	handful	happy	
halcyon	handicap	harangue	
hale	handicraft	harass	
half-caste	handily	harbour harbor	
half-hearted	handiwork	hard	
hall	handkerchief	hard-earned	
hallmark	handle	harden	

85

harder	harsh	hay
hardest	harshly	hazard
hard-hearted	harvest	hazardous
hardier	has	haze
hardiest	hash	hazily
hardly	haste	haziness
hardness	hasten	hazy
hardship	hastily	he
hardware	hasty	head
hardwood	hat	headache
hardy	hatch	headland
hare	hatchet	headlight
hark	hate	headline
harm	hateful	headlong
harmful	hatefully	headmaster
harmfully	hatred	headmistress
harmless	haughtily	headquarters
harmonious	haughty	headstrong
harmoniously	haul	headway
harmonize	haunt	heal
harmony	have	health
harness	haven	healthful
harp	havoc	healthier
harrow	hawk	healthiest

healthy	heavenly	helmet
heap	heavier	help
hear	heaviest	helpful
heard	heavily	helpfully
hearer	heaviness	helpless
hearsay	heavy	helplessly
hearse	heavyweight	helplessness
heart	Hebrew	helter-skelter
heartbroken	heckle	hem
heartfelt	hectic	hemisphere
hearth	hectically	hemp
heartily	hedge	hen
heartless	heed	hence
heartlessly	heedful	henceforth
heartrending	heedless	hence-forward
hearty	heel	her
heat	height	herald
heater	heir	heraldry
heath	heiress	herb
heathen	heirloom	herbaceous
heather	held	herbalist
heatwave	hell	herd
heave	hello	here
heaven	helm	hereabouts

hereafter	hesitant	highland
hereby	hesitantly	highlight
hereditary	hesitate	highly
heredity	hesitation	high-minded
here*in*	heterogeneous	highness
herinafter	hew	high-pitched
hereof	hewn	highroad
hereon	hexagon	high-spirited
hereto	heyday	highway
heretofore	hiatus	hike
herewith	hibernation	hilarious
heritage	hid	hilarity
hermetic	hidden	hill
hermetically	hide	hillside
hermit	hidebound	hilt
hero	hideous	him
heroic	hierarchy	himself
heroically	high	hinder
heroine	highbrow	hindrance
heroism	high-class	Hindu Hindoo
herring	higher	hinge
hers	highest	hint
herself	high-handed	hip
hesitancy	high-heeled	hire

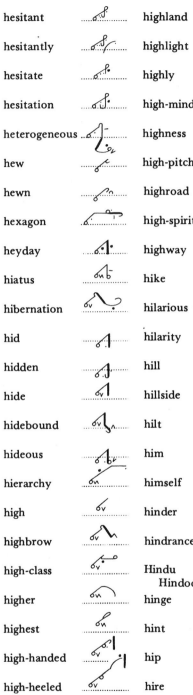
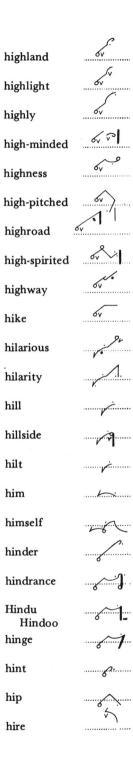

88

his	hoist	honesty
hiss	hold	honey
historian	holder	honeymoon
historic	hold-up	honorary
historical	hole	honour honor
historically	holiday	honourable honorable
history	holiness	honourably honorably
hit	hollow	hood
hitch	holly	hoodwink
hither	holocaust	hoof
hither*to*	holy	hook
hive	homage	hoop
hoard	home	hoot
hoarder	homecoming	hop
hoarse	homeless	hope
hoarsely	homely	hopeful
hoax	homesick	hopefully
hobble	homestead	hopefulness
hobby	homeward	hopeless
hobnob	homicide	hopelessly
hockey	homily	hopelessness
hod	homogeneous	horizon
hoe	honest	horizontal
hog	honestly	horizontally

horn	hostel	how
hornet	hostess	however
horrible	hostile	howl
horribly	hostility	howsoever
horrid	hot	hub
horrific	hotchpotch	huckleberry
horrify	hotel	huckster
horror	hothouse	huddle
horse	hotter	hue
horseback	hottest	huff
horsehair	hound	hug
horseman	hour	huge
horse-power	hourly	hugely
horse-racing	house	hulk
horticulture	household	hull
hose	householder	hum
hosiery	housekeeper	human
hospitable	housekeeping	humane
hospitably	housewarming	humanely
hospital	housewife	humanitarian
hospitality	housework	humanity
hospitalization	hovel	humanly
host	hover	humble
hostage	hovercraft	humbly

90

humbug	hunter	hydro-dynamics
humid	hurdle	hydro-electric
humidifier	hurl	hydrogen
humidity	hurrah	hygiene
humiliate	hurricane	hygienic
humiliation	hurry	hygienically
humility	hurt	hymn
humorist	hurtful	hyphen
humorous	husband	hypnotism
humorously	husbandry	hypocrisy
humour humor	hush	hypocrite
hump	husk	hypocritical
hunch	husky	hypothesis
hundred	hustings	hypothetic
hundredth	hustle	hypothetical
hundredweight	hustler	hypothetically
hung	hut	hysteria
hunger	hybrid	hysterical
hungry	hydraulic	hysterically
hunt	hydraulically	hysterics

I

I	idle	illogical
ice	idly	illogically
iceberg	idolatry	ill-timed
icebox	idolize	illuminate
ice-cream	idyllic	illumination
icicle	if	illumine
icy	ignite	ill-used
idea	ignition	illusion
ideal	ignominious	illusory
idealism	ignoramus	illustrate
idealist	ignorance	illustration
idealistic	ignorant	illustrative
idealistically	ignorantly	illustrator
ideally	ignore	illustrious
identical	ill	ill-will
identification	illegal	image
identify	illegally	imagery
identity	illegible	imaginary
idiocy	illegitimate	imagination
idiom	illicit	imaginative
idiosyncrasy	illiterate	imaginatively
idiot	ill-natured	imagine
idiotic	illness	imbecile

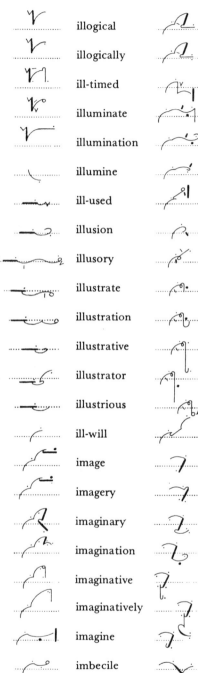
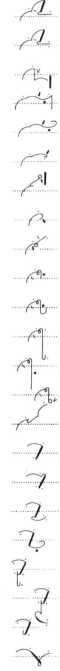

imitate	immorality	impel
imitation	immorally	impend
immaculate	immortal	imperative
immaterial	immortality	imperatively
immature	immovable	imperceptible
immeasurable	immune	imperfect
immeasurably	immunity	imperfection
immediate	imp	imperfectly
immediately	impact	imperial
immemorial	impair	imperialism
immense	impart	imperialist
immensely	impartial	imperishable
immensity	impartiality	impersonal
immerse	impartially	impersonation
immersion	impassable	impertinence
immigrant	impatience	impertinent
immigration	impatient	impertinently
imminent	impatiently	imperturbable
immobile	impeach	impervious
immoderate	impeccable	impetuous
immoderately	impeccably	impetuously
immodest	impecunious	impetus
immodestly	impede	impinge
immoral	impediment	implacable

93

implacably		impoverish		imprudent	
implausible		impracticable		imprudently	
implement		impractical		impudence	
implemen-tation		impregnable		impudent	
implicate		impregnate		impulse	
implication		impress		impulsive	
implicit		impression		impulsively	
implicitly		impressionable		impure	
implore		impressive		impurity	
imply		impressively		*in*	
impolite		imprint		inability	
impolitely		imprison		inaccessible	
import		imprisonment		inaccuracy	
importance		improbability		inaccurate	
important		improbable		inaccurately	
importer		impromptu		inactive	
impose		improper		inactivity	
imposition		improperly		inadequate	
impossibility		improve		inadequately	
impossible		improvement		inanimate	
imposter		improvident		inapplicable	
impotence		improvisation		inappropriate	
impotent		improvise		inappropriately	
impound		imprudence		inarticulate	

94

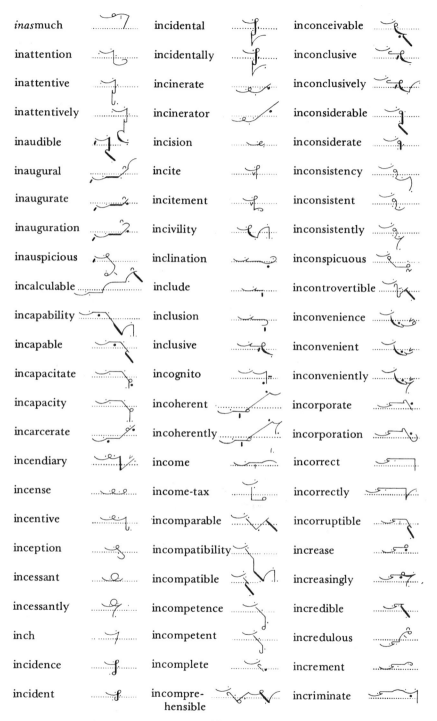

*inas*much	incidental	inconceivable
inattention	incidentally	inconclusive
inattentive	incinerate	inconclusively
inattentively	incinerator	inconsiderable
inaudible	incision	inconsiderate
inaugural	incite	inconsistency
inaugurate	incitement	inconsistent
inauguration	incivility	inconsistently
inauspicious	inclination	inconspicuous
incalculable	include	incontrovertible
incapability	inclusion	inconvenience
incapable	inclusive	inconvenient
incapacitate	incognito	inconveniently
incapacity	incoherent	incorporate
incarcerate	incoherently	incorporation
incendiary	income	incorrect
incense	income-tax	incorrectly
incentive	incomparable	incorruptible
inception	incompatibility	increase
incessant	incompatible	increasingly
incessantly	incompetence	incredible
inch	incompetent	incredulous
incidence	incomplete	increment
incident	incompre- hensible	incriminate

95

incubator	index	indiscriminate
incur	indicate	indiscriminately
incurable	indication	indispensable
indebted	indicative	indispose
indebtedness	indicator	indisputable
indecent	indices	indistinct
indecently	indict	indistinctly
indecision	indictment	individual
indeed	indifference	individually
indefatigable	indifferent	indivisible
indefensible	indifferently	indolent
indefinite	indigenous	indoor
indefinitely	indigestible	induce
indelible	indigestion	inducement
indelicate	indignant	induction
indemnify	indignantly	indulge
indemnity	indignation	indulgence
indent	indignity	indulgent
indentation	indirect	indulgently
independence	indirectly	industrial
independent	indiscernible	industrialist
independently	indiscreet	industrialization
indescribable	indiscreetly	industrious
indestructible	indiscretion	industry

inedible		infancy	infirmity
inefficiency		infant	inflame
inefficient		infantile	inflammable
inefficiently		infantry	inflammation
inelegant		infatuate	inflate
inept		infatuation	inflation
ineptitude		infect	inflexible
inequality		infection	inflict
inert		infectious	infliction
inertia		infer	*influence*
inescapable		inference	*influential*
inestimable		inferior	*influentially*
inevitable		inferiority	influenza
inexact		infernal	influx
inexcusable		inferno	inform
inexhaustible		infest	informal
inexpensive		infidelity	informality
inexperience		infiltrate	informally
inexpert		infinite	informant
inexplicable		infinitely	*information*
inexpressible		infinitive	informative
infallible		infinity	informer
infamous		infirm	infrequent
infamy		infirmary	infrequently

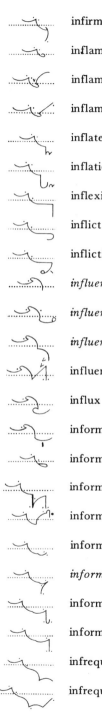

97

infringe		initial		innocent	
infringement		initially		innocently	
infuriate		initiate		innovation	
infuse		initiation		innumerable	
ingenious		initiative		inoculate	
ingenuity		inject		inopportune	
ingot		injection		inopportunely	
ingrain		injunction or		inorganic	
ingratiate		injure		input	
ingratitude		injurious		inquest	
ingredient		injury		inquisitive	
inhabit		injustice		inquisitively	
inhabitant		ink		inroad	
inhale		inlaid		insane	
inhere		inland		insanitary	
inherent		inlet		insanity	
inherit		inmate		insatiable	
inheritance		inmost		inscribe	
inheritor		inn		inscriber	
inhibition		innate		inscription	
inhospitable		innately		inscrutable	
inhuman		inner		insect	
inhumanly		innermost		insecticide	
iniquity		innocence		insecure	

98

insecurely	insistently	instigator
insecurity	insolence	instil(l)
insemination	insolent	instinct
insensible	insolently	instinctive
insensitive	insoluble	instinctively
inseparable	insolvent	institute
insert	insomnia	institution
insertion	inspect	instruct
inset	inspection	instruction
inside	inspector	instructive
insight	inspiration	instructor
insignia	inspire	instrument
insignifi- cance	instability	instrumental
insignifi- cant	install	insubordination
insignifi- cantly	installation	insubstantial
insincere	instalment installment	insufferable
insincerely	instance	insufficient
insincerity	instant	insufficiently
insinuate	instantaneous	insular
insinuation	instantly	insulate
insipid	instead	insulation
insist	instep	insulator
insistence	instigate	insulin
insistent	instigation	insult

insurable		intent		intermission	
insurance		intention		intermittent	
insure		intentional		inter-mittently	
insurgent		intently		intermix	
insurmount-able		inter		intern	
insurrection		interact		internal	
intact		intercede		international	
intake		intercept		internee	
integral		interchange		internment	
integrate		interchangeable		interpret	
integrity		intercourse		interpretation	
intellect		interdepart-mental		interpreter	
intellectual		interest		interrogate	
intelligence		interfere		interrogation	
intelligent		interference		interrupt	
intelligently		interim		interruption	
intelligible		interior		intersect	
intemperance		interlocking		intersection	
intend		interloper		intersperse	
intense		interlude		interval	
intensely		intermediary		intervene	
intensify		intermediate		intervention	
intensity		intermin-able		interview	
intensive		inter-mingle		intestate	

100

intestine		introvert		investigator	
intimacy		intrude		investment	
intimate		intrusion		investor	
intimately		intuition		invigilate	
intimation		intuitive		invigorate	
intimidate		intuitively		invincible	
intimidation		inundate		inviolable	
into		invade		inviolate	
intolerable		invalid		invisible	
intolerance		invalidate		invitation	
intolerant		invaluable		invite	
intonation		invariable		invoice	
intoxicate		invasion		invoke	
intravenous		invent		involuntary	
intrepid		invention		involve	
intricacy		inventor		involvement	
intricate		inventory		invulnerable	
intricately		inverse		inward	
intrigue		inversely		inwardly	
intrinsic		invert		iodine	
intrinsically		invertebrate		iota	
introduce		invest		irascible	
introduction		investigate		irate	
introductory		investigation		ire	

101

iris	irrepressible	*is*	
irksome	irreproachable	island	
iron	irresistible	isle	
ironical	irresolute	isolate	
ironmonger	irrespective	isolation	
irony	irrespectively	issue	
irrational	irresponsibility	isthmus	
irreconcilable	irresponsible	*it*	
irrecoverable	irrespons-ibly	italic	
irredeemable	irretrievable	italicize	
irrefutable	irreverent	itch	
irregular	irreverently	item	
irregularity	irrevocable	iterate	
irregularly	irrigate	itinerant	
irrelevance	irrigation	itinerary	
irrelevant	irritable	its	
irrelevantly	irritant	itself	
irremovable	irritate	ivory	
irreparable	irritation	ivy	

J

jab		jealousy		jigsaw	
jack		jeans		jingle	
jacket		jeer		jitters	
jade		jelly		job	
jag		jeopardize		jobber	
jagged		jeopardy		jobbing	
jaguar		jerk		jockey	
jail		jerry-built		jocose	
jailbird		jersey		jocular	
jailer jailor		jest		jocularly	
jam		jet		jog	
jamboree		jet-propelled		join	
jangle		jetsam		joiner	
janitor		jettison		joinery	
January		jetty		joint	
jar		Jew		jointed	
jargon		jewel		jointly	
jaundice		jeweller jeweler		joint-stock	
jaunt		jewellery jewelry		joist	
jaunty		Jewess		joke	
jauntily		Jewish		jollity	
jaw		jibe		jolly	
jealous		jig		jolt	

103

jostle		judder		jungle	
jot		judge		junior	
journal		judgment judgement		junk	
journalism		judicial		junta	
journalist		judicially		juridical	
journalistic		judicious		jurisdiction	
journalize		judiciously		jurisprudence	
journey		judo		jurist	
jovial		jug		juror	
jovially		juggle		jury	
jowl		juggler		just	
joy		jugular		justice	
joyful		juice		justifiable	
joyfully		July		justifiably	
joyous		jumble		justification	
joyously		jumbo		justify	
jubilant		jump		justly	
jubilantly		jumper		jut	
jubilation		junction	or.	jute	
jubilee		juncture	or.	juvenile	
Judaism		June		juxtaposition	

K

kaleidoscope		kick		kindred	
kangaroo		kicker		kine	
keel		kid		king	
keen		kidnap		kingdom	
keener		kidnapper kidnaper		king-pin	
keenest		kidney		king-post	
keenly		kill		kingship	
keep		kiln		kink	
keeper		kilogram		kinsfolk	
keepsake		kilometre kilometer		kinship	
keg		kilowatt		kinsman	
kennel		kilowatt-*hour*		kiss	
kept		kilt		kit	
kerb		kin		kitchen	
kernel		kind		kite	
kerosene		kinder		kitten	
kettle		kindergarten		kitty	
key		kindest		klaxon	
keyboard		kind-hearted		knack	
keyhole		kind-heartedly		knave	
keynote		kindle		knead	
keypunch		kindly		knee	
khaki		kindness		kneel	

105

		knock		knowingly	
knell		knocker		knowledge	
knew		knock-kneed		knowledgeable	
knife		knock-out		known	
knife-edge		knoll		knuckle	
knight		knot		kopeck	
				kopek	
knit		knotty		kosher	
knives		know		kraal	
knob		know-how		kudos	

106

L

label		lament		laryngitis	
laboratory		lamentable		lash	
laborious		laminated		lass	
labour labor		lamp		last	
labourer laborer		lance		lastly	
lace		land		latch	
lacerate		landlord		late	
lack		landowner		lat(e)ish	
lacquer lacker		landscape		lately	
lad		lane		latent	
ladder		language		later	
laden		languid		lateral	
ladle		lantern		latest	
lady		lap		lathe	
lag		lapel		lather	
lager		lapse		Latin	
laid		larch		latitude	
lain		lard		latter	
lair		larder		latterly	
laity		*large*		laud	
lake		*largely*		laudable	
lamb		*larger*		laugh	
lame		*largest*		laughter	

107

launch	lazy	least	
laundry	lead (metal)	leather	
laurel	lead	leave	
lavatory	leaden	lecture	
lavender	leader	lecturer	
lavish	leadership	led	
lavishly	leaf	ledge	
law	leaflet	ledger	
lawful	leafy	leek	
lawfully	league	leeway	
lawless	leak	left	
lawn	leakage	lefthanded	
lawsuit	leaky	leg	
lawyer	lean	legacy	
lax	leant	legal	
laxative	leap	legality	
lay	leapt	legalize	
layer	learn	legally	
layman	learnèd	legend	
layout	learner	legendary	
laze	learnt	legibility	
laziest	lease	legible	
lazily	leasehold	legion	
laziness	leash	legislate	

legislation	lest	library
legislative	let	licence / license
legislator	lethal	licencee / licensee
legislature	lethargy	lick
legitimacy	letter	lid
legitimate	lettuce	lie
leisure	level	lien
leisurely	lever	lieu
lemon	leverage	lieutenant
lemonade	levity	life
lend	levy	lifetime
lender	liability	lift
length	liable	ligature
lengthen	liaison	light
lengthy	liar	lightening
lenient	libel	lighter
leniently	libellous / libelous	lightest
lens	liberal	lighthearted
lent	liberality	lighthouse
less	liberally	lightly
lessen	liberate	lightning
lesser	liberation	like
lesson	liberty	likeable / likable
lessor	librarian	likelihood

109

likely	lint	litigate	
liken	lion	litigation	
likeness	lioness	litre	
likewise	lip	litter	
lilt	liquefy	little	
limb	liqueur	live, *v*	
limbless	liquid	live, *adj*	
lime	liquidate	liveable livable	
limit	liquidation	livelihood	
limitation	liquidator	lively	
limitless	liquor	liver	
limp	lisp	livery	
limpid	list	livestock	
line	listen	livid	
lineage	listener	lizard	
lineal	listless	load	
linen	lit	loaf	
liner	literal	loafer	
linger	literally	loam	
linguist	literary	loan	
liniment	literate	loath loth	
link	literature	loathe	
linoleum	lithe	loathsome	
linseed	lithography	loaves	

lob		loiter		loot		
lobby		loll		lop		
local		lone		loquacious		
locality		loneliness		lord		
localize		lonely		lore		
locally		lonesome		lorry		
locate		long		lose		
location		longer		loser		
loch lock locker		longest		loss		
locket		longhand		lot		
locomotion		longitude		lotion		
locomotive		longitudinal		lottery		
locum		long-lived		lotus		
lodge		longstanding		loud		
loft		long-suffering		louder		
loftily		long-term		loudest		
lofty		look		lounge		
log		lookout		lout		
loggerheads		loom		lovable		
logic		loop		love		
logical		loophole		loveless		
logically		loose		loveliness		
loin		loosely		lovely		
		loosen		lover		

111

lovingly	ludicrous	lure	
low	lug	lurid	
lower, *adj*	luggage	lurk	
lower, *v*	lugubrious	luscious	
lowest	lukewarm	lush	
lowland	lull	lust	
lowly	lullaby	lustily	
loyal	lumbago	lustre	
loyalty	lumber	luster	
		lusty	
lozenge	luminous	lute	
lubricant	lump	luxuriance	
lubricate	lunacy	luxuriant	
lubrication	lunar	luxuriate	
lucid	lunatic	luxurious	
luck	lunch	luxury	
luckier	luncheon	lymph	
luckless	lung	lynch	
lucky	lunge	lyric	
lucrative	lurch	lyrical	

112

M

Ma	magnificence	make
mace	magnificent	maker
machine	magnificently	makeshift
machinery	magnify	make-up
machinist	magnitude	malady
mad	mahogany	malaria
madam madame made	maid	male
	maiden	malevolent
madly	mail	malice
madman	maim	malicious
madness	main	maliciously
magazine	mainland	malign
magic	mainly	malignant
magician	mainspring	malleable
magistrate	mainstay	mallet
magnanimous	maintain	malt
magnate	maintenance	maltreat
magnesium	maisonette	Mama Mamma
magnet	maize	mammal
magnetic	majestic	mammoth
magnetism	majesty	man
magnetize	major	manacle
magneto	majority	manage

113

manageable	mankind	margin
management	manly	marine
manager	manner	mariner
manageress	manoeuvre manoeuver	marital
managerial	manor	maritime
mandate	manpower	mark
mandatory	mansion	marker
mane	manslaughter	market
manfully _or_	mantel	marketable
manger	mantle	marketplace
mangle	manual	maroon
manhandle	manufacture	marriage
manhole	manufacturer	marrow
manhood	manure	marry
mania	manuscript	marsh
maniac	many	marshal
manicure	map	martial
manifest	maple	martyr
manifestation	mar	martyrdom
manifesto	marauder	marvel
manifold	marble	marvellous marvelous
manila	March (march)	Marxist
manipulate	mare	mascot
manipulation	margarine	masculine

114

mash		mathematical		meadow	
mason		mathematically		meagre meager	
masonic		mathematician		meal	
masonry		mathematics		mealtime	
masquerade		matinee		mean	
mass		matriculate		meander	
massacre		matriculation		meaningless	
massage		matrimonial		meant	
massive		matrimony		meantime	
mast		matron		meanwhile	
master		matter		measurable	
masterful		mattress		measure	
masterly		mature		measurement	
masterpiece		maturity		meat	
mastery		maul		mechanic	
mat		mauve		mechanical	
match		maxim		mechanically	
matchless		maximum		mechanism	
mate		May (may)		mechanization	
material		may*be*		mechanize	
materialistic		mayonnaise		medal meddle	
materialize		mayor		media	
maternal		maze		medi(a)eval	
maternity		me		medial	

115

mediate		memoir		merciless	
mediation		memorable		mercy	
medical		memoranda		mere	
medicated		memoran-dum		merely	
medicinal		memorial		merge	
medicine		memorize		merger	
mediocre		memory		merit	
mediocrity		men		merriment	
meditate		menace		merry	
meditation		mend		mesh	
medium		menfolk		mesmerize	
medley		menial		mess	
meek		meningitis		message	
meet		mental		messenger	
melancholy		mentality		Messrs	
mellow		mention		met	
melodious		mentor		metal	
melody		menu		metamor-phosis	
melon		mercantile		metaphor	
melt		mercenary		metaphorically	
member		merchandise		mete	
membership		merchant		meteor	
membrane		merciful		meteoric	
memento		mercifully		meteorology	

116

metre		middle		mil(e)age		milestone
meter		middle-aged		milestone		
method		middle-class		militant		
methodical		middleman		military		
Methodist		midge		militate		
methylated		midget		militia		
meticulous		midnight	*or*	milk		
metric		midst		milkman		
metropolis		midsummer		milky		
metropolitan		midway		mill		
mettle		midwestern		miller		
mice		midwife		millimetre		
Michaelmas		midwinter		milliner		
microbe		mien		millinery		
microbiology		might		million		
microcosm		mighty		millionaire		
microfilm		migraine		millpond		
micrometer		migrant		mime		
micronometer		migrate		mimic		
microphone		migratory		mince		
microscope		mild		mincemeat		
microscopic		mildew		mind		
mid		mildly		mindful		
midday		mile		mine		

117

minefield		mirth		mislaid	
miner		mirthful		mislead	
mineral		misapprehension		mismanage	
mingle		misappropriation		misplace	
miniature		misbehave		misprint	
minimal		misbehaviour misbehavior		mispronounce	
minimize		miscellaneous		misquote	
minimum		mischief		misrepresent	
minister		mischievous		misrepresentation	
ministerial		misconceive		miss	
ministry		misconception		missile	
minor		misconduct		mission	
minority		misconstrue		missionary	
minster		miscreant		missive	
minstrel		misdemeanour misdemeanor		misspell	
mint		misdirect		misstatement	
minus		misery		mist	
minute, *n & v*		misfit		mistake	
minute, *adj*		misfortune		mistaken	
miracle		misgiving		mistook	
miraculous		misguided		mistress	
mirage		mishap		mistrust	
mire		misinform		misty	
mirror		misinterpret		misunderstand	

118

misunderstood	modern	money
misuse, *v & n*	modernization	mongrel
mite	modernize	monitor
mitigate	modest	monk
mitigation	modesty	monkey
mitre	modification	monogram
mix	modify	monograph
mixer	modulate	monolithic
mixture	Mohammedan	monoplane
mnemonic	moist	monopolize
moan	moisten	monopoly
moat	moisture	monosyllabic
mob	mole	monotonous
mobile	molecule	monotony
mobility	molest	Monotype
mobilization	molestation	monsoon
mock	molten	monster
mockery	momentarily	monstrosity
mode	momentary	monstrous
model	momentous	month
moderate, *n & adj*	monarch	monthly
moderate, *v*	monastery	monument
moderately	Monday	monumental
moderation	monetary	monumentally

119

mood		mortal	motor-car
moodily		mortality	motor-coach
moody		mortar	motor-cycle
moon		mortgage	motorist
moonlight		mortgagee	motorway
moonshine		mortgager mortgagor	mottled
moor		mortification	motto
moorland		mortify	mould mold
mop		moss	mouldy moldy
moped, *n*		most	moult
moral		mostly	mound
morale		motel	mount
moralist		moth	mountain
morality		mother	mountaineer
morbid		motherhood	mountainous
more		mother-*in*-law	mourn
*more*over		motherland	mourner
morgue		motif	mournful
morn		motion	mournfully
morning		motionless	mourning
moron		motivate	mouse
morrow		motive	moustache mustache
morse		motley	mouth
morsel		motor	mouthful

120

mouthpiece		multiply		musician		
mov(e)able		multitude		must		
move		Mum		mustard		
movement		mumble		muster		
mover		Mummy		musty		
mow		munch		mute		
mower		mundane		mutilate		
mown		municipal		mutilation		
Mr		municipality		mutiny		
Mrs		mural		mutter		
much		murder		mutton		
muck		murderer		mutual		
mud		murderess		muzzle		
muddle		murderous		my		
muddy		murky		myself		
muff		murmur		mysterious		
muffle		muscle		mystery		
mule		muscular		mystic		
mull		muse		mystify		
multi-coloured		museum		mystique		
multilateral		mushroom		myth		
multiple		music		mythology		
multiplication		musical		mythological		

121

N

nag		national		navigate	
nail		nationality		navigation	
naive		nationalization		navigator	
naked		nationalize		navy	
name		nationally		nay	
nameless		nationwide		near	
namely		native		nearby	
napalm		nativity		nearer	
napkin		natural		nearest	
narcissus		naturalist		nearly	
narcotic		naturalization		neat	
narrate		naturalize		neatly	
narrative		naturally		nebulous	
narrator		nature		necessarily	
narrow		naught		necessary	
narrower		naughty		necessitate	
narrowest		nausea		necessitous	
narrowly		nauseating		necessity	
narrow-minded		nautical		neck	
nasal		naval		nectar	
nasty		nave		need	
natal		navel		needful	
nation		navigable		needle	

122

needless		neither		newcomer		
needlessly		nephew		newer		
needlewoman		nephritis		newest		
needlework		nepotism		newfangled		
needy		nerve		newly		
nefarious		nervous		news		
negation		nervously		newsagent		
negative		nest		newscaster		
neglect		nestle		newspaper		
neglectful		net		newsprint		
		nett				
negligé		nettle		next		
negligence		network		nib		
negligent		neuralgia		nibble		
negligently		neurasthenia		nice		
negligible		neurosis		nicely		
negligibly		neurotic		nicer		
negotiable		neuter		nicest		
negotiate		neutral		nicety		
negotiation		neutrality		niche		
negress		neutralize		nick		
negro		never		nickel		
neigh		nevermore		nickname		
neighbour		nevertheless		niece		
neighbor						
neighbourhood	or	new		niggardly		

123

nigh	noiseless	nook
night	noiselessly	noon
nightly	noisily	noonday
nil	noisy	no-one
nimble	nomad	noose
nine	nomen-clature	nor
nineteen	nominal	normal
nineteenth	nominally	normally
ninetieth	nominate	north
ninety	nomination	north-east
ninth	nominative	north-easter
nip	nominee	north-eastern
nipple	non-appearance	northerly
nitrate	nonchalant	northern
nitric	nonchalantly	northerner
nitrogen	non-committal	northward
no	non-committally	northwest
nobility	non-conformist	north-westerly
noble	nondescript	north-western
nobly	none	nose
nobody	nonentity	nostalgia
nocturnal	nonplussed	nostril
nod	nonsense	not
noise	nonsensical	notability

124

notable		novel		nullity		
notary		novelist		numb		
notation		novelty		number		
notch		November		numeral		
note		novice		numerate		
noteworthy		now		numerical		
nothing		nowadays		numerous		
notice		nowhere		nun		
noticeable		noxious		nuptials		
noticeably		nozzle		nurse		
notification		nuance		nursery		
notify		nub		nurture		
notion		nuclear		nut		
notoriety		nucleus		nutriment		
notorious		nude		nutrition		
notoriously		nudge		nutritious		
notwithstanding		nudity		nutritive		
nought		nugget		nutshell		
noun		nuisance		nuzzle		
nourish		null		nylon		
nourishment		nullify		nymph		

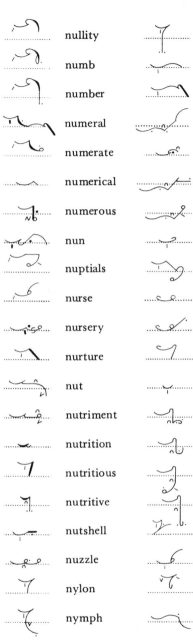

125

O

O, Oh	obligatory	obstetrics
oaf	oblige	obstinacy
oak	oblique	obstinate
oar	obliterate	obstinately
oasis	oblivion	obstreperous
oath	oblivious	obstruct
oatmeal	oblong	obstruction
oats	obnoxious	obstructive
obduracy	oboe	obtain
obedience	obscene	obtainable
obedient	obscure	obtrude
obediently	obscurity	obtrusive
obelisk	obsequious	obtrusively
obese	observance	obtuse
obesity	observant	obviate
obey	observation	obvious
obituary	observatory	obviously
object	observe	occasion
objection	observer	occasional
objectionable	obsession	occident
objective	obsolescence	occidental
objectively	obsolete	occult
obligation	obstacle	occupancy

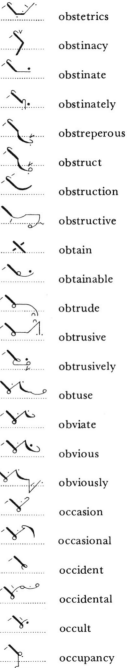
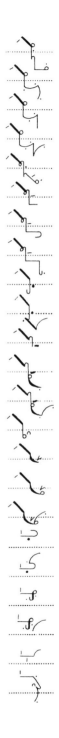

126

occupant	offence offense	oil-well
occupation	offend	oily
occupy	offender	ointment
occur	offensive	okay
occurrence	offensively	old
ocean	offer	older
o'clock	offhand	oldest
octagon	office	old-fashioned
octane	officer	olive
octave	official	omelette
octavo	officially	omen
October	officiate	ominous
oculist	officious	omission
odd	officiously	omit
oddity	offset	omnibus
oddment	offspring	omniscient
ode	often	omnivorous
odious	ogre	*on*
odorous	oil	once
odour odor	oil-field	one
of	oil-fired	onerous
off	oil-rig	oneself
offal	oilskin	one-sided
offchance	oil-tanker	one-way

127

onion		oppose		orb	
onlooker		opposite		orbit	
only		opposition		orchard	
onset		oppress		orchestra	
onslaught		oppression		orchid	
onward		oppressive		ordain	
ooze		oppressively		ordeal	
opaque		oppressor		order	
open		optic		orderly	
opener		optical		ordinance	
openly		optician		ordinarily	
opera		optimism		ordinary	
operate		optimistic		ordnance	
operatic		optimistically		ore	
operation		option		organ	
operative		optional		organic	
operator		opulent		organically	
operetta		or		organist	
opinion		oracle		organization	
opium		oral		organize	
opponent		orange		organizer	
opportune		oration		orgy	
opportunely		orator		orient	
opportunity		oratory		oriental	

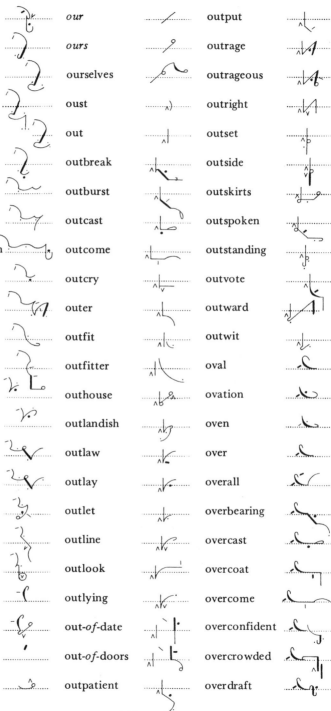

orientation	our	output
origin	ours	outrage
original	ourselves	outrageous
originality	oust	outright
originally	out	outset
originate	outbreak	outside
ornament	outburst	outskirts
ornamental	outcast	outspoken
ornamentation	outcome	outstanding
ornate	outcry	outvote
ornithology	outer	outward
orphan	outfit	outwit
orthodox	outfitter	oval
oscillate	outhouse	ovation
oscillation	outlandish	oven
ostensible	outlaw	over
ostensibly	outlay	overall
ostentatious	outlet	overbearing
osteopath	outline	overcast
ostracize	outlook	overcoat
other	outlying	overcome
otherwise	out-*of*-date	overconfident
ought	out-*of*-doors	overcrowded
ounce	outpatient	overdraft

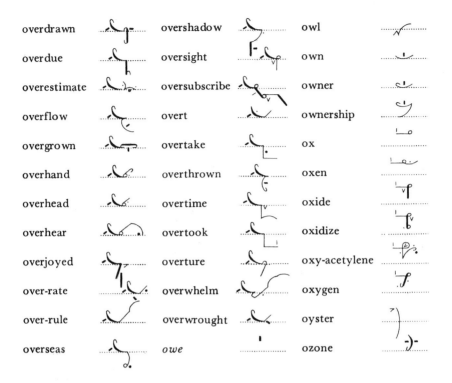

overdrawn	overshadow	owl	
overdue	oversight	own	
overestimate	oversubscribe	owner	
overflow	overt	ownership	
overgrown	overtake	ox	
overhand	overthrown	oxen	
overhead	overtime	oxide	
overhear	overtook	oxidize	
overjoyed	overture	oxy-acetylene	
over-rate	overwhelm	oxygen	
over-rule	overwrought	oyster	
overseas	*owe*	ozone	

P

Pa		painlessly		pan
pace		painstaking		panacea
pacific		paint		pancreas
pacifist		painter		pandemonium
pacify		pair		pander
pack		pal		pane
package		palace		panegyric
packer		palatable		panel
packet		palate		pang
pact		palatial		panic
pad		pale		panoply
paddle		pall		panorama
paddock		palliative		pant
padlock		pallid		pantomime
pagan		pallor		pantry
page		palm		Papa
pageant		palpable		papacy
pageantry		palpably		papal
pail		palpitate		paper
pain		palpitation		par
painful		paltry		parable
painfully		pamper		parachute
painless		pamphlet		parade

131

paradise	parish	partiality
paradox	parishioner	partially
paradoxical	parity	participant
paradoxically	park	participate
paraffin	parlance	participation
paragon	parley	participle
paragraph	parliament	particle
parallel	parliamentary	particular *ar*
paralyse paralyze	parlour parlor	particularly *ar*
paralysis	parlous	partisan
paramount	parochial	partition
paraphrase	parody	partly
parasite	parole	partner
parcel	paroxysm	partnership
parch	parquet	partook
parchment	parrot	party
pardon	parry	pass
pare	parsimonious	passable
parent	parsimoniously	passage
parentage	parsnip	passenger
parental	parson	passer-by
parenthesis	part	passion
parenthetical	partake	passionate
parenthetically	partial	passionately

passive	pathway	payee
passively	patience	payer
Passover	patient	payload
passport	patiently	paymaster
past	patriot	payment
paste	patriotic	payroll
pastel	patriotically	pea
pasteurize	patriotism	peace
pastime	patrol	peaceable
pastor	patron	peaceably
pastoral	patronage	peaceful
pastry	patronize	peacefully
pasture	patter	peach
pasty	pattern	peak
pat	paucity	peal
patch	pauper	peanut
patent	pause	pear
patentee	pave	pearl
patently	pavement	peasant
paternal	pavilion	peat
path	paw	pebble
pathetic	pawn	peck
pathetically	pay	pectoral
pathos	payable	peculation

peculiar	pelt	penultimate
peculiarity	pen	penurious
peculiarly	penal	penury
pecuniary	penalty	people
pedagogic	penance	pep
pedagogue	pence	pepper
pedal	pencil	per
pedant	pendant	per annum
pedantic	pending	perceive
peddle	pendulum	per cent
pedestal	penetrate	percent
pedestrian	penetration	percentage
pediatric	penicillin	perceptible
pedigree	peninsula	perceptibly
pedlar peddler	penitent	perception
peek	penitentiary	perceptive
peel	penknife	perceptively
peep	pennant	perch
peer	penniless	percolator
peerless	penny	percussion
peevish	pension	perdition
peevishly	pensioner	peremptorily
peg	pensive	peremptory
pejorative	penthouse	perennial

perennially		perishable		persecute	
perfect		perjure		persecution	
perfection		perjury		persecutor	
perfectionist		permanency		perseverance	
perfectly		permanent		persevere	
perfidy		permanently		persist	
perforate		permeate		persistence	
perform		permeation		persistent	
performance		permissible		persistently	
performer		permission		person	
perfume		permissive		personal	
perfunc- torily		permissively		personality	
perfunctory		permit		personally	
perhaps		permutation		personalty	
peril		pernicious		personifi- cation	
perilous		perpen- dicular		personnel	
perilously		perpe- trate		perspective	
perimeter		perpetual		perspicacious	
period		perpetually		perspicacity	
periodic		perpetuate		perspicuous	
periodical		perpetuity		perspicuity	
periodically		perplex		perspiration	
peripatetic		perplexity		perspire	
perish		perquisite		persuade	

135

persuasion		petitioner		philology	
persuasive		petrify		philosopher	
persuasively		petrol		philosophical	
pertain		petroleum		philosophically	
pertinacity		petticoat		philosophy	
pertinent		pettifogging		phlebitis	
perturb		petty		phlegmatic	
perusal		petulant		phlegmatically	
peruse		petulantly		phone	
pervade		pewter		phonetic	
perverse		phantom		phonetically	
perversely		pharmacist		phoney	
pervert		pharmacy		phosphorescent	
peseta		phase		phosphorous	
pessimism		phenomena		photo	
pessimist		phenomenal		photocopy	
pessimistic		phenomenally		photogenic	
pest		phenomenon		photograph	
pester		phial		photographer	
pestilence		philanthropic		photographic	
pestilent		philanthropist		photography	
pet		philanthropy		photostat	
petal		philharmonic		phrase	
petition		philistine		physical	

136

physically		pig		pipe		
physician		pigeon		pipeline		
physicist		pigeonhole		piper		
physics		pigment		piquant		
physiotherapist		pigmy		pique		
physique		pile		piracy		
pianist		pilfer		pirate		
piano		pilgrim		pistol		
pianoforte		pilgrimage		piston		
piastre		pill		pit		
pick		pillar		pitch		
picket		pillow		pitcher		
pickle		pilot		piteous		
picnic		pin		pith		
pictorial		pincers		pithy		
pictorially		pinch		pitiable		
picture		pine		pitiful		
picturesque		pink		pitifully		
picturesquely		pinnacle		pittance		
pie		pint		pity		
piece		pioneer		pivot		
pier		pious		pivotal		
pierce		piously		placard		
piety		pip		placate		

place		plastic		plebeian		
placid		plate		plebiscite		
plagiarism		plateau		pledge		
plague		platform		pleni- potentiary		
plaid		platinum		plenteous		
plain		platitude		plentiful		
plainer		plausibility		plentifully		
plainest		plausible		plenty		
plainly		play		pleurisy		
plaintiff		player		pliable		
plaintive		playful		pliers		
plait		playground		plight		
plan		playmate		plod		
plane		playroom		plot		
planet		plaything		plough plow		
planetarium		playwright		pluck		
plank		plea		plug		
plankton		plead		plum		
plant		pleasant		plumage		
plantation		pleasantly		plumb		
planter		please		plumber		
plaque		pleasurable		plume		
plaster		pleasure		plump		
plasterer		pleat		plunder		

138

plunge		pointlessly		pompous
plunger		poise		pompously
plural		poison		pond
plus		poisonous		ponder
plush		poke		ponderous
ply		polar		pontificate
pm		pole		pontoon
pneumatic		polemic		pony
pneumonia		police		pool
poach		policeman		poor
poacher		policy		poorer
pocket		polish		poorest
pod		polite		poorly
poem		politely		pop
poet		political		Pope
poetess		politically		poplar
poetic		politician		poplin
poetical		politics		populace
poetically		poll		popular
poetry		pollute		popularity
poignant		pollution		population
point		polytechnic		porcelain
pointer		polythene		porch
pointless		pomp		pore

139

pork		possess		postponement	
porous		possession		postscript	
porpoise		possessive		postulate	
porridge		possessor		postulant	
port		possibility		posture	
portable		possible		posy	
portal		possibly		pot	
portend		post		potash	
portent		postage		potassium	
portentous		postal		potato	
portentously		postcard		potent	
porter		postdated		potentate	
portfolio		poster		potential	
portico		posterior		potentially	
portion		posterity		pothole	
portrait		postgraduate		potion	
portraiture		posthumous		potter	
portray		posthumously		pottery	
pose		postman		pouch	
poser		postmark		poultice	
poseur		postmaster		poultry	
position		post-mortem		pounce	
positive		postpaid		pound	
positively		postpone		poundage	

pour		prayer		preclude	
pout		preach		precocious	
poverty		preacher		preconception	
powder		preamble		preconcerted	
power		precarious		predatory	
powerful		precariously		predecessor	
powerfully		precast		predestined	
powerless		precaution		predetermined	
practicability		precautionary		predicament	
practicable		precede		predicate	
practical		precedence		predict	
practically		precedent		predictably	
practice practise		precept		prediction	
practitioner		precinct		predominance	
pragmatic		precious		predominant	
pragmatically		precipice		predominantly	
prairie		precipitant		pre-eminent	
praise		precipitantly		pre-eminently	
praiseworthy		precipitate		pre-empt	
prance		precipitous		preface	
prank		précis		prefect	
prate		precise		prefer	
prattle		precisely		preferable	
pray		precision		preferably	

141

preference	prepaid	preside
preferential	preparation	presidency
preferment	preparatory	president
prefigure	prepare	presidential
prefix	prepay	press
pregnant	preponderance	pressure
prehistoric	preposition	prestige
prejudge	preposterous	prestressed
prejudice	prerequisite	presumably
prejudicial	prerogative	presume
prejudicially	Presbyterian	presumption
prelate	prescient	presumptive
preliminary	prescribe	presumptuous
prelude	prescription	presuppose
premature	presence	pretence pretense
prematurely	present	pretend
premeditate	presentable	pretentious
premeditation	presentably	pretext
premier	presentation	pretty
premise	presentiment	prevail
premises	presently	prevalence
premium	preservation	prevalent
premonition	preservative	prevaricate
preoccupied	preserve	prevent

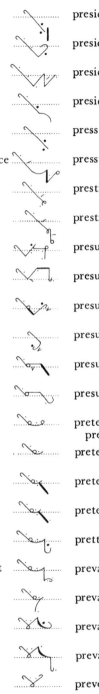
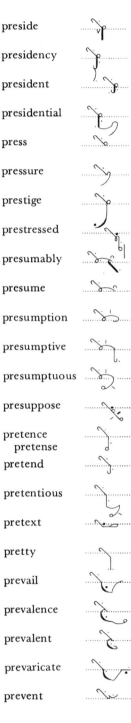

preventative		primrose		probably	
prevention		primus		probate	
preventive		prince		probation	
preview		princess		probationary	
previous		principal		probe	
previously		principality		probity	
pre-war		principally		problem	
prey		principle		problematic	
price		print		procedural	
priceless		printer		procedure	
prick		prior		proceed	
prickle		priority		process	
pride		prism		procession	
priest		prison		proclaim	
prig		prisoner		proclamation	
prim		privacy		procrastinate	
primarily		private		procreate	
primary		privately		proctor	
primate		privation		procure	
prime		privilege		prod	
primer		prize		prodigal	
primeval		pro		prodigous	
primitive		probability		prodigously	
primogeniture		probable		prodigy	

143

produce		pro-forma		prolong	
producer		profound		promenade	
product		profoundly		prominence	
production		profuse		prominent	
productive		profusion		prominently	
productively		progeny		promiscuous	
productivity		prognosis		promise	
profane		prognosticate		promissory	
profanity		programme program		promontory	
profess		progress		promote	
profession		progressive		promoter	
professional		progressively		promotion	
professionalism		prohibit		promotional	
professor		prohibition		prompt	
professorship		prohibitive		promptitude	
proffer		prohibitively		promptly	
proficiency		project		promulgate	
proficient		projection		prone	
proficiently		projector		prong	
profile		proletarian		pronoun	
profit		proletariat		pronounce	
profitable		proliferate		pronouncement	
profitably		prolific		pronunciation	
profligate		prologue		proof	

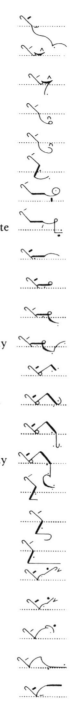
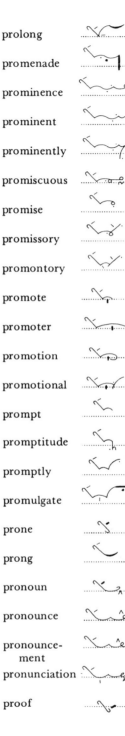

144

prop	proposition	protect
propaganda	propound	protection
propagate	proprietary	protectionist
propel	proprietor	protective
propeller	propriety	protectively
propensity	propulsion	protector
proper	prorogue	protectorate
properly	prosaic	protégé
property	proscribe	protein
prophecy	prose	protest
prophesy	prosecute	Protestant
prophet	prosecution	protestation
prophetic	prosecutor	protocol
prophetically	prospect	protracted
propitiate	prospective	protrude
propitious	prospectively	protuberant
propitiously	prospectus	proud
proponent	prosper	proudly
proportion	prosperity	provable
proportional	prosperous	prove
proportionate	prosperously	proven
propor- tionately	prostrate	proverb
proposal	prostration	proverbial
propose	protagonist	proverbially

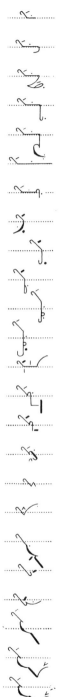

provide		pseudo		pulley	
providence		pseudonym		pullover	
provident		psychiatric		pulmonary	
province		psychic		pulp	
provincial		psychological		pulpit	
provision		psychologist		pulse	
provisional		psychology		pumice	
provisionally		psychotherapy		pump	
provocation		ptomaine		pun	
provocative		puberty		punch	
provocatively		public		punctilious	
provoke		publication		punctual	
provost		publicist		punctuality	
prow		publicity		punctually	
prowess		publicize		punctuate	
prowl		publicly		punctuation	
proximity		publish		puncture	
proxy		publisher		pundit	
prudence		pudding		pungent	
prudent		puddle		punish	
prudently		puerile		punishment	
prune		puff		punitive	
pry		pugnacious		punt	
psalm		pull		puny	

146

pup		purity		pursuit		
pupil		purloin		pus		
puppet		purple		push		
puppy		purport		put		
purchase		purpose		putative		
purchaser		purposely		putrid		
pure		purr		putt		
purely		purse		putty		
purgatory		purser		puzzle		
purge		pursuance		pyjamas		
purification		pursuant		pylon		
purify		pursue		pyramid		
Puritan		pursuer		pyre		

Q

quack	quarter	questioner
quadrangle	quarterdeck	questionnaire
quadrant	quarterly	queue
quadrille	quartern	quibble
quadruped	quarters	quick
quadruplicate	quartet	quicken
quagmire	quarto	quicker
quail	quartz	quickest
quaint	quash	quickly
quaintly	quasi	quicksand
quake	quaver	quicksilver
quaker	quay	quickwitted
qualification	queen	quid pro quo
qualify	queer	quiescent
quality	queerly	quiet
qualm	quell	quieter
quandary	quench	quietly
quantity	querulous	quietness
quarantine	query	quietus
quarrel	quest	quilt
quarrelsome	question	quinine
quarry	questionable	quintal
quart	questionably	quintessence

quintet		quitter		quorum	
quip		quiver		quota	
quire		quixotic		quotation	
quit		quiz		quote	
quite		quizzical		quoter	
quittance		quoit		quotient	

R

rabbi	radioactive	rainy
rabbit	radiogram	raise
rabble	radiologist	raisin
rabid	radiotherapy	rake
rabies	radish	rally
race	radium	ram
racehorse	radius	ramble
racer	raffle	rambler
racial	raft	ramification
racially	rafter	ramp
rack	rag	rampage
racket	rage	rampant
racy	ragged	rampart
radar	raid	ramshackle
radiance	rail	ran
radiant	railroad	ranch
radiantly	railway	rancid
radiate	raiment	rancour rancor
radiation	rain	rand
radiator	rainbow	random
radical	raincoat	rang
radically	rainfall	range
radio	rainproof	ranger

150

rank	rat(e)able	reach
rankle	ratepayer	react
ransack	rather	reaction
ransom	ratification	reactionary
rant	ratify	reactivate
rap	rating	read
rapacious	ratio	readable
rapacity	ration	reader
rape	rational	readier
rapid	rationalization	readily
rapidity	rationally	readiness
rapidly	rattle	readjust
rapport	raucous	readjustment
rapt	ravage	readmission
rapture	rave	readmit
rare	ravenous	ready
rarity	ravine	reaffirm
rascal	ravish	real
rash	raw	realism
rashly	ray	realist
raspberry	rayon	realistic
rat	raze	realistically
ratchet	razor	reality
rate	re	realization

151

realize		rebellion		recess	
really		rebellious		recession	
realm		rebound		recharge	
realty		rebuff		recipe	
ream		rebuild		recipient	
reap		rebuilt		reciprocal	
reappear		rebuke		reciprocate	
reappearance		rebut		reciprocity	
reappoint		recalcitrant		recital	
reappointment		recall		recitation	
reapportion		recant		recite	
rear		recapitulate		reckless	
rearrange		recapitulation		reckon	
rearrangement		recapture		reclaim	
reason		recast		reclamation	
reasonable		recede		recline	
reasonably		receipt		recluse	
reassemble		receive		recognition	
reassert		receiver		recognizance	
reassurance		recent		recognize	
reassure		recently		recoil	
rebate		receptacle		recollect	
rebel, *n & adj*		reception		recollection	
rebel, *v*		receptive		recommence	

152

recommend	recruit	redress
recommendation	rectangular	reduce
recompense	rectify	reduction
reconcile	rectitude	redundant
reconciliation	rector	reed
recondite	rectum	reef
reconnaissance	recumbent	reek
reconnoitre reconnoiter	recuperate	reel
reconquer	recuperation	re-elect
reconsider	recur	re-election
reconsideration	recurrence	re-enact
reconstitute	recurrent	re-entrant
reconstruct	red	re-establish
reconstruction	redeem	re-examine
record	redemption	refectory
recorder	red-handed	refer
recount	red-hot	referee
recoup	redistribute	reference
recourse	redolent	referendum
recover	redouble	refine
recoverable	redoubt	refinement
recovery	redoubtable	refiner
recrimination	redound	refinery
recrudescence	redraft	reflation

153

reflect	refute	regrettably
reflection	regain	regular
reflective	regal	regularity
reflectively	regale	regularly
reflex	regard	regulate
reform	regardless	regulation
reformation	regency	regulator
reformatory	regenerate	regulatory
reformer	regent	regurgitate
refraction	regime	rehabilitate
refractory	regimen	rehabilitation
refrain	regiment	rehash
refresh	regimental	rehearsal
refreshment	region	rehearse
refrigerate	regional	rehouse
refrigeration	regionally	reign
refrigerator	register	reimburse
refuge	registrar	reimbursement
refugee	registration	rein
refund	registry	reindeer
refurbish	regret	reinforce
refusal	regretful	reinstate
refuse	regretfully	reinstatement
refutation	regrettable	reiterate

154

reiteration		reliably		remind	
reject		reliance		reminder	
rejection		reliant		reminisce	
rejoice		relic		reminiscence	
rejoinder		relief		reminiscent	
rejuvenate		relieve		remiss	
relapse		religion		remission	
relate		religious		remit	
relation		relinquish		remittance	
relationship		relish		remnant	
relative		reluctance		remonstrance	
relatively		reluctant		remonstrate	
relax		reluctantly		remorse	
relaxation		rely		remorseless	
relay		remain		remote	
release		remainder		remotely	
relegate		remand		removable	
relent		remark		removal	
relentless		remarkable		remove	
relentlessly		remarkably		remover	
relevancy		remedial		remunerate	
relevant		remedy		remuneration	
reliability		remember		remunerative	
reliable		remembrance		remuneratively	

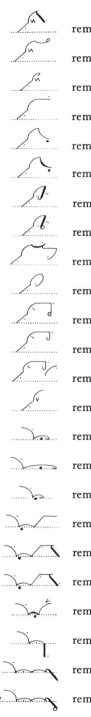

155

renaissance	repeatedly	representative
rend	repel	reprieve
render	repellant	reprimand
rendezvous	repent	reprisal
renegade	repentance	reproach
renewal	repentant	reproachful
renounce	repercussion	reproachfully
renovate	repertoire	reprobate
renovation	repertory	reproduce
renown	repetition	reproduction
rent	repine	reprove
rental	replenish	reptile
renunciation	replete	republic
reorientate	repletion	republican
reorganiza-tion	replica	repudiate
repair	reply	repudiation
reparable	report	repugnance
reparation	reporter	repugnant
repartee	repose	repulse
repast	repository	repulsion
repatriate	reprehend	repulsive
repayment	reprehen-sible	reputable
repeal	represent	reputation
repeat	representation	repute

156

request	residual	respectable
requiem	residuary	respectably
require	residue	respectful
requirement	resign	respectfully
requisite	resignation	respective
requisition	resignedly	respectively
requite	resilience	respiration
rescind	resilient	respirator
rescue	resin	respiratory
rescuer	resist	respire
research	resistance	resplendent
resemblance	resistant	resplendently
resemble	resolute	respond
resent	resolutely	response
resentful	resolution	responsibility
resentment	resolve	responsible
reservation	resonant	responsibly
reserve	resort	responsive
reservoir	resoundingly	restart
reside	resource	restaurant
residence	resourceful	restaurateur
residency	resourcefully	restful
resident	respect	restfully
residential	respectability	restitution

157

restive		retaliatory		return	
restless		retard		returnable	
restoration		retch		reunion	
restorative		retention		reunite	
restore		retentive		revaluation	
restrain		reticence		reveal	
restraint		reticent		revel	
restrict		retina		revelation	
restriction		retinue		revelry	
restrictive		retire		revenge	
result		retirement		revenue	
resultant		retort		reverberate	
resume		retouch		reverberation	
resumé		retrace		revere	
resumption		retract		reverence	
resurgence		retreat		reverend	
resurrection		retrench		reverent	
resuscitate		retrenchment		reversal	
resuscitation		retribution		reverse	
retail		retrieve		reversible	
retailer		retroactive		reversion	
retain		retrograde		revert	
retaliate		retrogressive		revetment	
retaliation		retrospect		review	

reviewer	rheumatism	right
revile	rhyme / rime	righteous
revise	rhythm	righteousness
revision	rib	rightful
revival	ribald	rightfully
revive	ribbon	right-hand
revocation	rice	rightly
revoke	rich	rigid
revolt	richer	rigidity
revolution	richest	rigorous
revolutionary	rid	rigorously
revolutionize	riddance	rigour / rigor
revolve	riddle	rile
revolver	ride	rim
revue	rider	rind
revulsion	ridge	ring
reward	ridicule	ringer
reword	ridiculous	ringlet
re-write	riding	rink
re-written	rife	rinse
rhapsody	riffraff	riot
rhetoric	rifle	rioter
rhetorical	rift	riotous
rheumatic	rig	rip

159

ripe
ripen
riper
ripest
riposte
ripple
rise
risen
risk
risky
rite
ritual
rival
rivalry
river
rivet
road
roadster
roadway
roam
roan
roar
roast
rob

robber
robbery
robe
robin
robot
robust
rock
rocker
rockery
rocket
rod
rode
rodent
roe
rogue
roguish
role
roll
roller
roman
romance
romantic
romantically
romp

romper
roof
roofless
rook
room
roomy
roost
rooster
root
rope
rosary
rose
roster
rostrum
rosy
rot
rota
rotary
rotate
rotation
rotatory
rote
rotor
rotten

rotund		rubber		rule	
rotundity		rubbish		ruler	
rouble		rubble		rum	
rouge		rubicund		rumble	
rough		rubric		ruminate	
roughen		ruby		rummage	
rougher		ruction		rumour rumor	
roughest		rudder		rump	
roughly		rude		rumple	
round		rudeness		run	
roundabout		rudiment		rung	
rouse		rudimentary		runner	
rout		rue		runway	
route		rueful		rupture	
routine		ruefully		rural	
rove		ruff		ruse	
rover		ruffian		rush	
row (a tier)		ruffle		rusk	
row (a noise)		rug		russet	
rowdy		rugged		rust	
royal		ruin		rustic	
royally		ruination		rusticate	
royalty		ruinous		rustle	
rub		ruinously		rustless	

rustproof		rut		ruthlessly
rusty		ruthless		rye

S

Sabbath	sahib	salute
sabbatical	said	salvage
sabotage	sail	salvation
saccharin(e)	sailor	salve
sack	saint	same
sacrament	saintly	sample
sacred	sake	sanatorium
sacrifice	salad	sanctify
sad	salary	sanctimonious
sadden	sale	sanction
saddle	saleable salable	sanctuary
sadist	salesman	sand
sadly	saleswoman	sandal
safe	salient	sandwich
safeguard	saline	sandy
safely	saliva	sane
safer	sallow	sanely
safest	salmon	sang
safety	saloon	sanguinary
sag	salt	sanguine
sagacious	salubrious	sanitarium
sagacity	salutary	sanitary
sage	salutation	sanitation

sanity	Saturday	scalpel
sank	sauce	scamp
sap	saucepan	scamper
sapphire	saucer	scan
sarcasm	saunter	scandal
sarcastic	sausage	scandalous
sarcastically	savage	scandalously
sardine	savagely	scant
sardonic	savagery	scantily
sash	save	scanty
sat	saviour	scapegoat
satanic	savour savor	scar
satchel	savoury	scarce
satellite	saw	scarcity
satiate	sawdust	scare
satin	sawn	scarf
satire	saxophone	scarlet
satirical	say	scathing
satisfaction	scab	scathingly
satisfactorily	scaffold	scatter
satisfactory	scald	scavenger
satisfy	scale	scene
saturate	scallop	scenery
saturation	scalp	scenic

164

scenically		scintillating		scratch	
scent		scissors		scrawl	
sceptic skeptic		scoff		scream	
sceptical skeptical		scold		screech	
scepticism skepticism		scoop		screed	
sceptre scepter		scope		screen	
schedule		scorch		screw	
schedule		score		screwdriver	
scheme		scorn		scribble	
schemer		scornful		scribe	
schism		scorpion		scrimmage	
schizophrenia		scotch		scrimp	
scholar		scotfree		script	
scholarly		scoundrel		scripture	
scholarship		scour		scroll	
scholastic		scourge		scrounge	
school		scout		scrub	
schoolhouse		scowl		scrum	
schooner		scraggy		scruple	
sciatica		scramble		scrupulous	
science		scrap		scrutinize	
scientific		scrape		scrutiny	
scientifically		scrapheap		scuffle	
scientist		scrappy		sculptor	

165

sculpture		seaworthy		secular	
scum		secede		secure	
scurrilous		secession		securely	
scurry		seclude		security	
scurvy		seclusion		sedan	
scuttle		second		sedate	
scythe		secondary		sedately	
sea		second-hand		sedentary	
seafaring		secondly		sediment	
seal		second-rate		sedition	
sea-level		secrecy		seditious	
sealing-wax		secret		see	
seam		secretarial		seed	
seaman		secretariat		seedling	
seance		secretary		seek	
sear		secrete		seem	
search		secretion		seemingly	
searcher		secretive		seemly	
searchingly		secretively		seen	
seashore		sect		seep	
season		sectarian		seer	
seasonable		section		seethe	
seasonal		sectional		segment	
seaweed		sector		segregate	

segregation	sell	sensitive
seismic	seller	sensitively
seize	selves	sensual
seizure	semantics	sent
seldom	semblance	sentence
select	semester	sentiment
selection	semicircle	sentimental
selective	semicolon	sentinel
selectively	seminar	sentry
self	seminary	separate, *adj*
self-centred	senate	separate, *v*
self-confident	senator	separation
self-conscious	send	separator
self-contained	sender	September
self-control	senile	sepulchre sepulcher
self-defence	senior	sequel
self-discipline	seniority	sequence
self-explanatory	sensation	sequester
self-help	sensational	sequestrate
selfish	sense	serenade
selfishly	senseless	serene
selfishness	senselessly	serenely
self-respect	sensibility	serenity
self-willed	sensible	serge

167

sergeant	seventeenth	shadowy	
serial	seventh	shaft	
series	seventieth	shaggy	
serious	seventy	shah	
seriously	sever	shake	
seriousness	several	shaken	
sermon	severally	shaker	
serpent	severance	shakier	
serrated	severe	shall	
servant	severely	shallow	
serve	severity	sham	
service	sew	shame	
serviceable	sewer	shameful	
serviceman	sewer	shamefully	
servile	sewerage	shameless	
servility	sewn	shamelessly	
servitude	sex	shampoo	
session	sexton	shank	
set	shabbily	shape	
settle	shabby	shapeless	
settlement	shack	shapely	
settler	shackle	share	
seven	shade	shareholder	
seventeen	shadow	shark	

168

sharp		shell		shirk	
sharpen		shellfish		shirt	
sharper		shelter		shiver	
sharpest		shelve		shoal	
sharply		shepherd		shock	
sharp-witted		sherbet		shod	
shatter		sheriff		shoddily	
shave		sherry		shoe	
shawl		shield		shoemaker	
she		shift		shoe-string	
sheaf		shiftless		shone	
shear		shifty		shook	
sheath		shilling		shoot	
sheathe		shimmer		shooter	
sheaves		shin		shop	
shed		shine		shore	
sheen		shingle		shorn	
sheep		shiny		short	
sheepish		ship		shortage	
sheepishly		shipbuilding		shortcoming	
sheer		shipment		shorten	
sheet		shipowner		shorter	
shekels		shipper		shortest	
shelf		shire		shorthand	

169

shortly		shrinkage		siege	
shortsighted		shrivel		sieve	
shortsightedly		shroud		sift	
short-term		shrub		sigh	
shot		shrug		sight	
should		shrunk		sight-seeing	
shoulder		shudder		sign	
shout		shuffle		signal	
shove		shun		signatory	
shovel		shunt		signature	
show		shut		signer	
shower		shutter		significance	
showmanship		shuttle		significant	
shown		shy		significantly	
showroom		shyly		signify	
shrank		sick		silence	
shred		sicken		silent	
shrew		sickle		silently	
shrewd		sickly		silhouette	
shriek		sickness		silicon	
shrill		side		silk	
shrimp		sidewalk		silkworm	
shrine		sideways		silly	
shrink		sidle		silo	

170

silt		sinew		sit		
silver		sinewy		site		
similar		sinful		situate		
similarity		sing		situation		
similarly		singe		six	6. or	
simile		singer		sixteen	16. or	
similitude		single		sixteenth	16. or	
simmer		singular		sixth	6. or	
simper		singularity		sixty	60. or	
simple		singularly		size		
simpler		sinister		sizeable		
simplest		sink		sizzle		
simpleton		sinner		skate		
simplicity		sinus		skater		
simplify		sip		skein		
simply		siphon		skeleton		
simulate		sir		sketch		
simultaneous		sire		ski		
sin		siren		skid		
since		sirloin		skiff		
sincere		sisal		skilful skillful		
sincerely		sister		skilfully		
sincerity		sister-*in*-law		skill		
sinecure		sisterly		skim		

171

skimp	slang	slept
skin	slant	slew
skinflint	slap	slice
skinny	slash	slick
skip	slate	slid
skipper	slaughter	slide
skirmish	slaughterhouse	slight
skirt	slave	slightly
skit	slavery	slim
skittle	slavish	slime
skulduggery	slavishly	sling
skulk	slay	slink
skull	slayer	slip
skunk	sledge	slipper
sky	sleek	slippery
skyscraper	sleep	slipshod
slab	sleeper	slit
slack	sleeplessness	slither
slacken	sleepwalking	sliver
slag	sleepy	slobber
slain	sleet	slog
slam	sleeve	slogan
slander	sleigh	slop
slanderous	slender	slope

slot	small	smoulder smolder
sloth	smaller	smudge
slothful	smallest	smug
slouch	smart	smuggle
slough (*a bog*)	smarten	smuggler
slovenly	smarter	smugly
slow	smartest	smut
slowly	smartly	snack
sludge	smash	snag
slug	smattering	snail
sluggard	smear	snake
sluggish	smell	snap
sluggishly	smile	snare
sluice	smilingly	snarl
slum	smirk	snatch
slumber	smith	sneak
slump	smock	sneer
slung	smoke	sneeringly
slur	smoker	sneeze
slush	smooth	sniff
slut	smoother	snigger
sly	smoothest	snip
slyly	smoothly	snivel
smack	smother	snob

173

snobbish		soccer		sole		
snobbishly		sociable		solecism		
snooker		social		solely		
snoop		socialism		solemn		
snore		socialist		solemnity		
snort		society		solemnization		
snout		sociology		solemnly		
snow		sock		solicit		
snowfall		socket		solicitor		
snowplough		sod		solicitude		
snowshoes		soda		solid		
snowstorm		sodden		solidarity		
snub		sodium		solidify		
snuff		sofa		solidity		
snug		soft		solidly		
so		soften		soliloquy		
soak		softly		solitary		
soap		soggy		solitude		
soar		soil		solo		
sob		solace		soloist		
sober		solar		solstice		
soberly		sold		solubility		
sobriety		solder	or	soluble		
so-called		soldier		solution		

174

solve

solvency

solvent

sombre
somber

some

somebody

somehow

someone

somersault

something

sometime

somewhat

somewhere

somnolent

son

song

son-in-law

sonnet

sonorous

soon

sooner

soonest

soot

soothe

sooty

sop

sophisticated

sophistication

sophistry

sophomore

soporific

soprano

sorcerer

sordid

sore

sorely

sorrow

sorrowful

sorry

sort

sought

soul

sound

sounder

soundest

soup

sour

source

sourly

south

southeast

southeastern

southern

southerner

southward

southwest

southwestern

souvenir

sovereign

sovereignty

sow (a pig)

sow (to scatter)

sower

sown

soya-bean

space

space-craft

spacious

spade

span

spangle

spaniel

175

spank		specialist		speed	
spanner		speciality		speedily	
spar		specialize		speedometer	
spare		specially		speedy	
sparingly	*or.*	specialty		spell	
spark		specie		spend	
sparkle		specific		spent	
sparrow		specifically		sphere	
sparse		specification		spherical	
sparsely		specify		sphinx	
sparsity		specimen		spice	
Spartan		speck		spicy	
spasm		speckle		spider	
spasmodic		spectacle		spike	
spasmodically		spectacular		spill	
spastic		spectator		spilt	
spat		spectre specter		spin	
spatter		spectrum		spinach	
spawn		speculate		spinal	
speak		speculation		spindle	
speaker		speculative		spindrier	
spear		speculator		spine	
spearhead		sped		spineless	
special		speech		spinster	

176

spiral		spokesman	sprint	
spire		sponge	sprite	
spirit		sponsor	sprout	
spiritedly		spontaneous	spruce	
spiritual		spontaneously	sprung	
spit		spool	spry	
spite		sporadic	spun	
spiteful		sporadically	spur	
spitefulness		sport	spurious	
splash		sportsman	spuriously	
splay		spot	spurn	
spleen		spotless	spurt	
splendid		spouse	spy	
splendidly		spout	squabble	
splendour splendor		sprain	squad	
splice		sprang	squadron	
splint		sprawl	squalid	
splinter		spray	squall	
split		spread	squalor	
splutter		spree	squander	
spoil		sprig	square	
spoilt		sprightly	squash	
spoke		spring	squat	
spoken		sprinkle	squaw	

177

squawk		staid		star		
squeak		stain		starboard		
squeal		stainless		starch		
squeamish		stair		stare		
squeamishly		stake		stark		
squeeze		stalactite		starkly		
squib		stalagmite		starling		
squint		stale		starry-*eyed*		
squire		stalk		star-spangled		
squirm		stall		start		
squirrel		stalwart		starter		
squirt		stamina		startle		
stab		stammer		starvation		
stability		stamp		starve		
stabilize		stampede		state		
stable		stance		statement		
stack		stand		statesman		
stadium		standard		static		
staff		standardization		station		
stag		standardize		stationary		
stage		standpoint		stationer		
stagger		standstill		stationery		
stagnant		stank		statistical		
stagnation		staple		statistically		

178

statistician	steel	steward
statistic	steep	stewardess
statue	steeple	stewardship
statuesque	steeply	stick
stature	steer	stickily
status	steerage	stiff
statute	stem	stiffen
statutory	stench	stifle
staunch	stencil	stigmatize
stave	stenographer	stile
stay	stenography	still
stead	step	stimulant
steadfast stedfast	stereo	stimulate
steadfastly	stereotyped	stimulation
steadily	sterile	stimulus
steady	sterility	sting
steak	sterilize	stingily
steal	sterling	stingy
stealth	stern	stink
stealthily	sternly	stint
stealthy	stet	stipend
steam	stetson	stipulate
steamer	stevedore	stipulation
steed	stew	stir

179

stirrup		stork		strap	
stitch		storm		strategically	
stock		story		strategy	
stockbroker		stout		stratification	
stockholder		stoutly		stratosphere	
stockist		stove		stratum	
stocktaking		stow		straw	
stoker		stowage		strawberry	
stole		straddle		stray	
stolen		straggle		streak	
stolid		straight		stream	
stomach		straighten		streamline	
stone		straight-forward		street	
stonily		strain		strength	
stood		strainer		strengthen	
stooge		strait		strenuous	
stool		straitlaced		strenuously	
stoop		strand		stress	
stop		strange		stretch	
stoppage		strangely		stretcher	
stopper		stranger		strew	
stopwatch		strangest		stricken	
storage		strangle		strict	
store		stranglehold		stricter	

180

strictest		strongly		stump		
strictly		strove		stun		
stricture		struck		stung		
stride		structural		stunt		
strident		structure		stupefaction		
stridently		struggle		stupefy		
strife		strum		stupendous		
strike		strung		stupendously		
striker		strut		stupid		
string		stub		stupidity		
stringency		stubble		stupor		
stringent		stubborn		sturdy		
stringently		stubbornly		stutter		
strip		stubbornness		sty		
stripe		stuck		style		
stripling		stud		stylish		
strive		student		styptic		
strode		studio		suave		
stroke		studious		subcommittee		
stroll		studiously		subconscious		
strong		study		subdue		
stronger		stuff		subject		
strongest		stultify		subjection		
stronghold		stumble		subjective		

181

subjectively		substantive		succumb	
subjunctive		substitute		such	
sublime		substitution		suck	
submission		subterfuge		suckle	
submit		subterranean		suction	
subordinate		subtle		sudden	
subpoena subpena		subtlety		suddenly	
subscribe		subtract		sue	
subscriber		subtraction		suède	
subscription		suburb		suet	
subsequent		suburban		suffer	
subsequently		subversion		sufferance	
subservient		subvert		suffice	
subserviently		subway		sufficiency	
subside		succeed		sufficient	
subsidence		success		sufficiently	
subsidiary		successful		suffix	
subsidize		successfully		suffocate	
subsidy		succession		suffocation	
subsist		successive		suffrage	
subsistence		successor		suffragette	
substance		succinct		sugar	
substantial		succinctly		suggest	
substantiate		succour succor		suggestion	

182

suggestive	summon	superiority
suicide	sump	superlative
suit	sumptuous	supernatural
suitability	sumptuously	supernumerary
suitable	sun	supersede
suite	Sunday	superstition
suitor	sunder	superstitious
sulky	sundry	supervise
sullen	sung	supervision
sulphate	sunk	supervisor
sulphide	sunken	supervisory
sulphona-mide	sunny	supper
sulphur	sup	supplant
sulphuric	super	supple
sulphurous	superannuation	supplement
sultan	superb	supplemental
sultry	superbly	supplemen-tary
sum	supercilious	suppliant
summarily	superficial	supplicant
summarize	superfluous	supplicate
summary	superhuman	supplication
summer	superintend	supplier
summer-house	superintendent	supply
summit	superior	support

supportable		surmount		sustenance	
supporter		surname		swagger	
suppose		surpass		swallow	
supposition		surplice		swam	
suppress		surplus		swamp	
suppression		surprise		swan	
supremacy		surrender		swap	
supreme		surreptitious		swarm	
supremely		surreptitiously		swarthy	
surcharge		surround		swathe	
sure		survey		sway	
surely		surveyor		swear	
surer		survival		sweat	
surest		survive		sweater	
surety		survivor		sweep	
surf		susceptible		sweeper	
surface		suspect		sweet	
surfeit		suspend		sweeten	
surge		suspense		sweeter	
surgeon		suspension		sweetest	
surgery		suspicion		sweetly	
surgical		suspicious		sweetness	
surly		suspiciously		swell	
surmise		sustain		swelter	

swept		swoop		symposium		
swerve		sword		symptom		
swift		swore		synagogue		
swifter		sworn		synchronize		
swiftest		swum		syncopation		
swiftly		swung		syndicate		
swill		syllable		synonym		
swim		syllabus		synonymous		
swimmer		symbol		synopsis		
swindle		symbolic		syntax		
swine		symbolically		synthesis		
swing		symbolize		synthetic		
swipe		symmetrical		syringe		
swirl		symmetry		syrup		
switch		sympathetic		system		
swivel		sympathize		systematic		
swollen		sympathy		systematical		
swoon		symphony		systematically		

T

tab	tactless	tame
table	tactlessly	tamper
tableau	tag	tan
tablecloth	tail	tandem
tablespoon	tail-end	tang
tablet	tail-light	tangent
tabloid	tailor	tangible
taboo	tailor-made	tangibly
tabular	tail-piece	tangle
tabulate	taint	tank
tabulation	take	tankard
tabulator	taken	tanker
tacit	take-off	tanner
tacitly	take-over	tantalize
taciturn	talcum	tantamount
tack	tale	tantrum
tackle	talent	tap
tact	talk	tape
tactful	talkative	taper
tactfully	talker	tape-recorder
tactically	tall	tapestry
tactician	tallow	tar
tactics	tally	tardily

186

tardiness		taught		tearful	
tardy		taunt		tearfully	
tare		taut		tease	
target		tautology		teaspoon	
tariff		tavern		technical	
tarmac		tawdry		technicality	
tarnish		tax		technically	
tarpaulin		taxable		technician	
tarry		taxation		technique	
tart		tax-collector		technology	
tartan		taxes		tedious	
tartar		tax-free		tediously	
tartaric		taxi		tedium	
task		taxidermy		teem	
taskmaster		taxpayer		teenager	
tassel		teach		teeth	
taste		teacher		teethe	
tasteful		teach-*in*		teetotal	
tastefully		team		teetotal(l)er	
tasteless		teamster		tele-communication	
tasty		team-work		telegram	
tatter		teapot		telegraph	
tattle		tear, *n*		telegraphic	
tattoo		tear, *v*		telegraphist	

187

telegraphy	temporarily	tent
telepathy	temporary	tentacle
telephone	tempt	tentative
telephonist	temptation	tentatively
teleprinter	ten	tenterhooks
telescope	tenable	tenth
teletype	tenacious	tenure
television	tenaciously	tepid
telex	tenacity	tepidly
tell	tenancy	term
teller	tenant	terminal
tell-tale	tend	terminate
temerity	tendency	termination
temper	tender	terminology
temperament	tenderly	terminus
tempera-mental	tendon	terrace
tempera-mentally	tendril	terrain
temperance	tenement	terrestrial
temperate	tenet	terrible
temperature	tenfold	terribly
tempest	tennis	terrier
tempestuous	tenor	terrific
temple	tense	terrifically
temporal	tension	terrify

188

territorial	texture	thence
territory	than	thenceforth
terror	thank	thence-forward
terrorist	thankful	theodolite
terse	thankfully	theological
tersely	thankfulness	theology
tertiary	thankless	theorem
test	thanks	theoretical
testament	thanksgiving	theoretically
testator	that	theorist
testatrix	thatch	theory
tester	thatcher	there
testify	thaw	thereabouts
testily	the	thereafter
testimonial	theatre theater	thereat
testimony	theatrical	thereby
testy	thee	therefore
tetanus	theft	therein
tetchy	their	thereof
tether	theirs	thereon
text	them	thereto
textbook	theme	thereupon
textile	themselves	therewith
textual	then	therm

thermo-dynamics	third	thoughtlessly
thermometer	third-rate	thoughtlessness
thermostat	thirst	thousand
these	thirsty	thousandfold
thesis	thirteen _or 13_	thousandth
they	thirtieth _or 30_	thrash
thick	thirty _or 30_	thread
thicken	_this_	threadbare
thicker	thistle	threat
thickest	thong	threaten
thicket	thorn	three
thickly	thorny	three-quarters
thief	thorough	thresh
thieves	thoroughbred	threshold
thigh	thoroughfare	threw
thimble	thoroughly	thrice
thin	those	thrift
thine	thou	thrifty
thing	though	thrill
think	thought	thrive
thinker	thoughtful	throat
thinly	thoughtfully	throb
thinner	thoughtfulness	throes
thinnest	thoughtless	throne

190

throng	tidily	time-saving	
throttle	tidings	time-server	
through	tidy	time-signal	
throughout	tie	time-switch	
throw	tier (a row)	timetable	
thrown	tiff	timid	
thrush	tiger	timidity	
thrust	tight	timidly	
thud	tighten	timorous	
thug	tightly	tin	
thumb	tightness	tincture	
thump	tigress	tinder	
thunder	tile	tinge	
thunderbolt	till	tingle	
thunderstorm	tillage	tinker	
Thursday	tilt	tinkle	
thus	timber	tinsel	
thwart	time	tint	
tick	time-bomb	tiny	
ticket	time-consuming	tip	
tickle	time-honoured	tippler	
ticklish	timekeeper	tipsy	
tidal	timeless	tirade	
tide	timely	tire	

191

tireless	tolerable	top
tiresome	tolerably	topaz
tiro tyro	tolerance	topic
tissue	tolerate	topical
titanic	toleration	topically
tithe	toll	topography
titivate	tomato	topple
title	tomb	torch
titter	tombstone	tore
tittle-tattle	tomorrow	torment
titular	ton	torn
to	tone	tornado
toad	tongs	torpedo
toast	tongue	torpid
tobacco	tonic	torrent
toboggan	tonight	torrential
today	tonnage	torrid
toe	tonsil	torso
toffee	*too*	tort
together	took	tortoise
toil	tool	tortuous
toilet	toot	torture
token	tooth	toss
told	toothache	tot

total		towpath		trail	
totalitarian		toxic		trailer	
totally		toy		train	
totem		trace		trainee	
totter		traceable		trainer	
touch		track		trait	
touchy		tract		traitor	
tough		tractable		tramp	
toughen		traction		trample	
tougher		tractor		tramway	
toughest		trade		trance	
toughness		trade-*in*		tranquil	
tour		trademark		tranquillity	
tourist		trader		tranquillizer	
tournament		tradesman		tranquilly	
tout		trades-union		transact	
tow		trade-union		transaction	
toward		tradition		transatlantic	
towards		traditional		transcend	
towel		traditionally		trans-continental	
tower		traffic		transcribe	
town		tragedy		transcript	
township		tragic		transcription	
townsman		tragically		transfer	

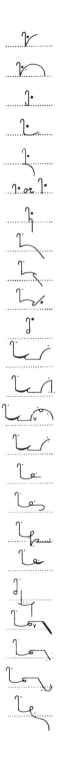

193

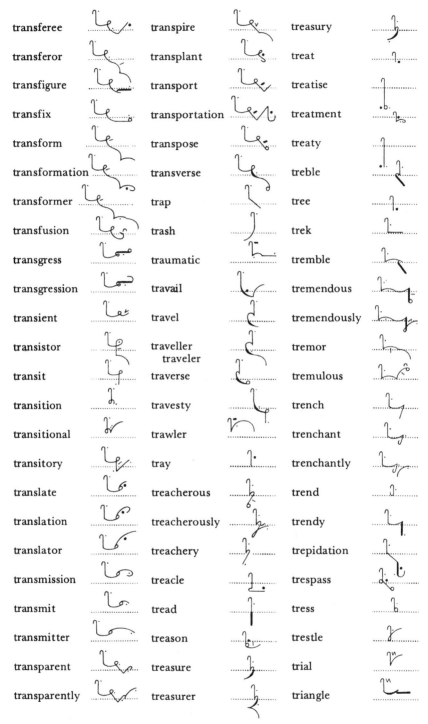

transferee	transpire	treasury
transferor	transplant	treat
transfigure	transport	treatise
transfix	transportation	treatment
transform	transpose	treaty
transformation	transverse	treble
transformer	trap	tree
transfusion	trash	trek
transgress	traumatic	tremble
transgression	travail	tremendous
transient	travel	tremendously
transistor	traveller	tremor
	traveler	
transit	traverse	tremulous
transition	travesty	trench
transitional	trawler	trenchant
transitory	tray	trenchantly
translate	treacherous	trend
translation	treacherously	trendy
translator	treachery	trepidation
transmission	treacle	trespass
transmit	tread	tress
transmitter	treason	trestle
transparent	treasure	trial
transparently	treasurer	triangle

194

triangular	triple	trounce	
tribal	triplets	troupe	
tribe	triplicate	trousers	
tribulation	tripod	trousseau	
tribunal	tripos	trout	
tribune	trite	trowel	
tributary	triumph	truant	
tribute	triumphant	truce	
trick	triumphantly	truck	
trickery	trivial	truckle	
trickle	triviality	truculence	
trickster	trivially	truculent	
tricky	trod	truculently	
trident	trodden	trudge	
trifle	trolley	true	
trigger	trombone	truffle	
trigonometry	troop	truism	
trill	trooper	truly	
trilogy	trophy	trump	
trim	tropical	trumpet	
trinket	trot	truncate	
trio	trouble	truncheon	
trip	troublesome	trundle	
tripe	trough	trunk	

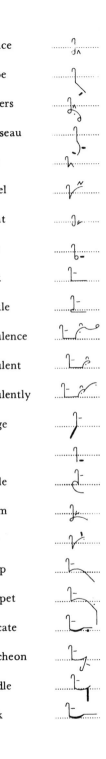

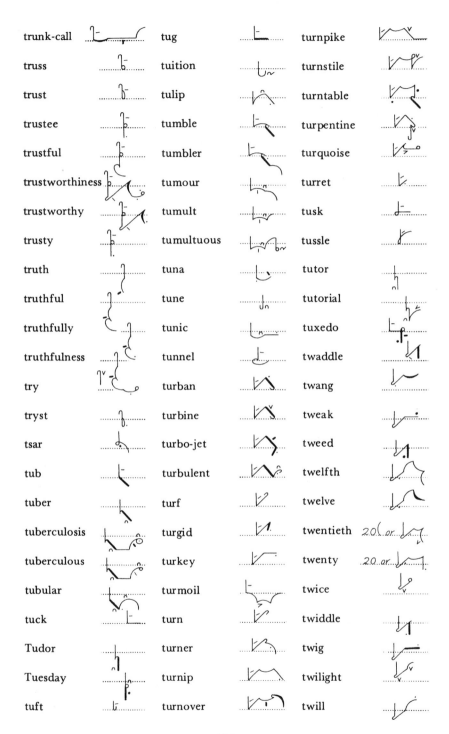

trunk-call	tug	turnpike	
truss	tuition	turnstile	
trust	tulip	turntable	
trustee	tumble	turpentine	
trustful	tumbler	turquoise	
trustworthiness	tumour	turret	
trustworthy	tumult	tusk	
trusty	tumultuous	tussle	
truth	tuna	tutor	
truthful	tune	tutorial	
truthfully	tunic	tuxedo	
truthfulness	tunnel	twaddle	
try	turban	twang	
tryst	turbine	tweak	
tsar	turbo-jet	tweed	
tub	turbulent	twelfth	
tuber	turf	twelve	
tuberculosis	turgid	twentieth	
tuberculous	turkey	twenty	
tubular	turmoil	twice	
tuck	turn	twiddle	
Tudor	turner	twig	
Tuesday	turnip	twilight	
tuft	turnover	twill	

twin		two-seater		typical	
twine		two-some		typically	
twinge		tycoon		typify	
twinkle		type		typist	
twirl		typecast		typographer	
twist		typewriter		typographical	
twit		typewriting		typography	
twitch		typewritten		tyrannical	
two		typhoid		tyranny	
two-faced		typhoon		tyrant	
twofold		typhus		tyre	

197

U

ubiquitous	unaccountable	unbalanced
udder	unaccustomed	unbearable
uglier	unacquainted	unbecoming
ugliest	unadaptable	unbeknown
ugly	unaffected	unbelievable
ukelele	unalterable	unbending
ulcer	unanimity	unbiased
ulterior	unanimous	unbleached
ultimate	unanimously	unblemished
ultimately	unanswerable	unbolt
ultimatum	unapproachable	unborn
ultra	unarmed	unbounded
ultramarine	unashamedly	unbreakable
ultra-violet	unasked	unbridled
umbilical	unassisted	unbroken
umbrage	unassuming	unburden
umbrella	unattached	unceasing
umpire	unattainable	uncertain
unabated	unattractive	unchallengeable
unable	unauthorized	unchanged
unabridged	unavailable	uncharitable
unacceptable	unavoidable	uncivilized
unaccom- panied	unaware	uncle

unclean	undaunted	understatement
uncomfortable	undecided	understood
uncommitted	undefended	understudy
uncommon	undefined	undertake
uncommuni-cative	undeniable	undertaken
uncomplaining	under	undertone
uncomplimen-tary	undercover	underwear
uncompromis-ing	undercurrent	underwriter
unconcern	undercut	undeserved
unconcernedly	underestimate	undesirable
unconditional	undergo	undeterred
unconfirmed	undergraduate	undeveloped
unconnected	underground	undid
unconscious	undergrowth	undignified
unconstitu-tional	underhand	undiluted
uncontrollable	underline	undiminished
unconventional	underlying	undischarged
uncorrected	undermine	undisclosed
uncouth	underneath	undiscovered
uncover	underrate	undisguised
uncultivated	undersigned	undismayed
uncut	undersize	undisturbed
undamaged	understand	undivided
undated	understandably	undoubted

undoubtedly	unfair	unguarded
undress	unfaithful	unhampered
undue	unfamiliar	unhappily
unduly	unfashionable	unhealthy
undying	unfasten	unheeded
unearned	unfavourable	unhesitatingly
unearth	unfeeling	unhindered
uneasy	unfinished	unhurt
uneconomic	unflinching	uniform
unedifying	unfold	uniformity
unemployed	unforeseeable	uniformly
unencumbered	unforeseen	unify
unenterprising	unforgettable	unilateral
unenviable	unforgivable	unimaginable
unequal	unfortunate	unimpaired
unequivocal	unfortunately	unimportant
unerring	unfounded	unimpressive
uneven	unfriendly	uninhibited
uneventful	unfruitful	uninspiring
unexampled	unfulfilled	uninsured
unexceptionable	unfurnished	unintelligible
unexpected	ungrammatical	unintentional
unexpectedly	ungrateful	uninterrupted
unfailing	ungrudgingly	union

200

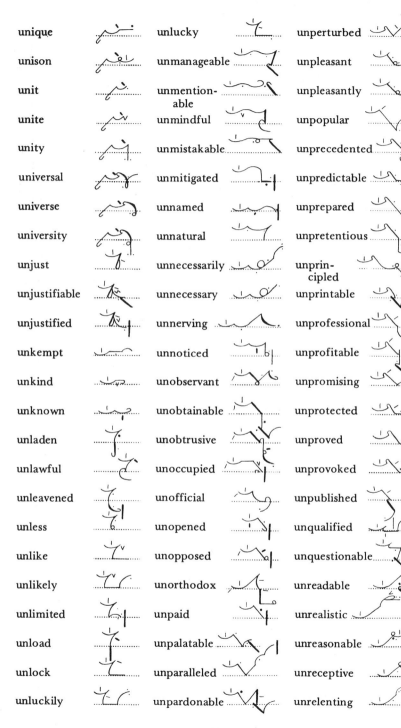

unique	unlucky	unperturbed
unison	unmanageable	unpleasant
unit	unmention-able	unpleasantly
unite	unmindful	unpopular
unity	unmistakable	unprecedented
universal	unmitigated	unpredictable
universe	unnamed	unprepared
university	unnatural	unpretentious
unjust	unnecessarily	unprin-cipled
unjustifiable	unnecessary	unprintable
unjustified	unnerving	unprofessional
unkempt	unnoticed	unprofitable
unkind	unobservant	unpromising
unknown	unobtainable	unprotected
unladen	unobtrusive	unproved
unlawful	unoccupied	unprovoked
unleavened	unofficial	unpublished
unless	unopened	unqualified
unlike	unopposed	unquestionable
unlikely	unorthodox	unreadable
unlimited	unpaid	unrealistic
unload	unpalatable	unreasonable
unlock	unparalleled	unreceptive
unluckily	unpardonable	unrelenting

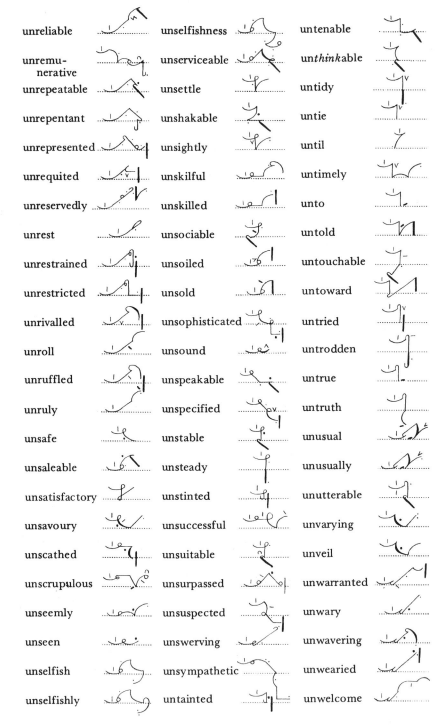

unreliable	unselfishness	untenable
unremu-nerative	unserviceable	un*think*able
unrepeatable	unsettle	untidy
unrepentant	unshakable	untie
unrepresented	unsightly	until
unrequited	unskilful	untimely
unreservedly	unskilled	unto
unrest	unsociable	untold
unrestrained	unsoiled	untouchable
unrestricted	unsold	untoward
unrivalled	unsophisticated	untried
unroll	unsound	untrodden
unruffled	unspeakable	untrue
unruly	unspecified	untruth
unsafe	unstable	unusual
unsaleable	unsteady	unusually
unsatisfactory	unstinted	unutterable
unsavoury	unsuccessful	unvarying
unscathed	unsuitable	unveil
unscrupulous	unsurpassed	unwarranted
unseemly	unsuspected	unwary
unseen	unswerving	unwavering
unselfish	unsympathetic	unwearied
unselfishly	untainted	unwelcome

202

unwell		upon		use	
unwholesome		upper		useful	
unwieldy		uppermost		usefulness	
unwilling		upright		useless	
unwise		uproar		uselessly	
unwittingly		uproot		uselessness	
unworldly		upset		usher	
unworthy		upshot		usual	
unwritten		upside-down		usually	
unyielding		upstairs		usurp	
up		upstart		utensil	
update		upwards		utility	
upgrade		uranium		utilize	
upheaval		urban		utmost	
upheld		urchin		Utopia	
uphill		urge		utter	
uphold		urgency		utterance	
upholster		urgent		utterly	
upholstery		urgently		uttermost	
upkeep		urn		uvula	
uplift		usable		uvular	

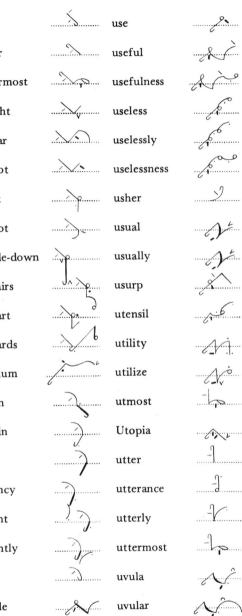
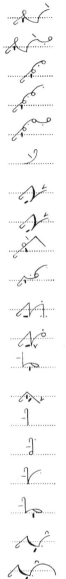

V

vacancy	valiantly	vapid
vacant	valid	vapour vapor
vacate	validity	variable
vacation	valise	variance
vaccinate	valley	variation
vaccination	valour valor	varicose
vaccine	valuable	variety
vacillate	valuation	various
vacuous	value	variously
vacuum	valueless	varnish
vacuum- cleaner	valuer	vary
vagabond	valve	vase
vagary	vamp	Vaseline
vagrancy	vampire	vassal
vagrant	van	vast
vague	vandal	vastly
vaguely	vandalism	vat
vain	vanguard	vault
vainly	vanilla	vaunt
vale	vanish	veal
valedictory	vanity	vector
valet	vanquish	veer
valiant	vantage	vegetable

204

vegetarian		venomous		veritable	
vegetation		vent		vermilion	
vehemence		ventilate		vermin	
vehement		ventilation		vernacular	
vehemently		ventilator		versatile	
vehicle		ventriloquist		versatility	
vehicular		venture		verse	
veil		venturesome		versify	
vein		venue		version	
veldt		veracity		verso	
vellum		verandah		versus	
velocity		verb		vertebrae	
velvet		verbal		vertebrate	
venal		verbally		vertical	
vend		verbatim		vertically	
vendetta		verbiage		vertigo	
vendor vender		verbose		verve	
veneer		verbosity		very	
venerable		verdant		vessel	
veneration		verdict		vest	
vengeance		verdure		vestibule	
venial		verge		vestige	
venison		verification		vestment	
venom		verify		vestry	

vet	viciously	villainous
veteran	vicissitude	villainously
veterinary	victim	villainy
veto	victimization	vim
vex	victor	vindicate
vexation	victorious	vindication
vexatious	victory	vindictive
via	victuals	vindictively
viable	video	vine
viaduct	vie	vinegar
vibrant	view	vineyard
vibrate	viewpoint	vintage
vibration	vigil	vinyl
vicar	vigilance	violation
vicarious	vigilant	violence
vicariously	vignette	violent
vice vise	vigorous	violently
vice-chairman	vigorously	violet
vice-chancellor	vigour vigor	violin
vice-president	vile	violinist
vice-principal	vilify	viper
vice versa	villa	virgin
vicinity	village	virile
vicious	villain	virility

206

virtual	vitality	volatile	
virtually	vitally	volcano	
virtue	vitamin	volition	
virtuoso	vitiate	volley	
virtuous	vitriolic	volt	
virulent	vituperative	voltage	
virus	vivacious	volubility	
visa	vivaciously	voluble	
visage	vivacity	volume	
viscount	vivid	voluminous	
viscous	vividly	voluntarily	
visibility	vixen	voluntary	
visible	vocabulary	volunteer	
visibly	vocal	voluptuous	
vision	vocalist	vomit	
visionary	vocally	voracious	
visit	vocation	voraciously	
visitor	vocational	vote	
visor	vociferous	voter	
vista	vociferously	vouch	
visual	vodka	voucher	
visualize	vogue	vouchsafe	
visually	voice	vow	
vital	void	vowel	

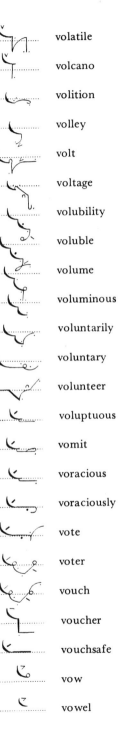

voyage	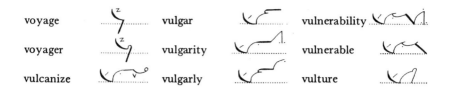	vulgar		vulnerability	
voyager		vulgarity		vulnerable	
vulcanize		vulgarly		vulture	

W

wad	wallet	warfare
wade	wallop	warily
wafer	wallow	warlike
waffle	wallpaper	warm
waft	walnut	warmer
wag	walrus	warmest
wage	waltz	warm-hearted
wager	wan	warmly
wagon waggon	wand	warmth
waif	wander	warn
wail	wane	warp
waist	wangle	warrant
waistline	want	warranty
wait	wanton	warren
waiter	wantonly	warrior
waitress	war	warship
waive	warble	wart
waiver	ward	wary
wake	warden	was
waken	warder	wash
walk	wardrobe	washer
walker	warehouse	washing-up
wall	wares	wasp

209

wastage		waxen		wearily
waste		way		wearisome
wasteful		waybill		weary
wastefully		wayfarer		weather
wastrel		waylay		weave
watch		wayside		weaver
watcher		wayward		web
watchful		we		wed
watchman		weak		wedding
water		weaken		wedge
waterfall		weaker		Wednesday
waterlogged		weakest		weed
watermark		weakly		week
watermelon		weakness		weekday
waterproof		weal		weekend
watershed		wealth		weekly
watertight		wealthier		weep
waterway		wealthiest		weigh
waterworks		wealthy		weight
watery		wean		weightily
watt		weapon		weighty
wave		wear		weird
wavy		wearable		welcome
wax		wearer		weld

210

welfare	westward	whereon
well	wet	wheresoever
well-balanced	whack	whereto
well-being	whale	whereupon
well-bred	wharf	wherever
well-disposed	wharfinger	wherewithal
well-informed	what	whether
well-known	whatever	which
well-meaning	whatsoever	whichever
well-meant	wheat	whiff
well-off	wheatsheaf	while
well-read	wheel	whilst
well-spoken	wheelbarrow	whim
well-timed	wheelchair	whimper
well-wisher	when	whimsical
welt	whence	whimsically
wench	whenever	whine
wend	where	whip
went	whereabouts	whirl
wept	whereas	whirlpool
were	whereby	whirlwind
west	wherefore	whisk
westerly	wherein	whisky whiskey
western	whereof	whisper

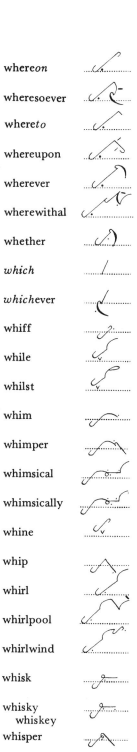

whist		wide		wilt	
whistle		widely		wily	
white		widen		win	
whitewash		wider		wince	
whither		widespread		winch	
whittle		widest		wind, *n*	
whiz		widow		wind, *v*	
who		widower		windmill	
*who*ever		width		window	
whole		wield		windscreen	
wholehearted		wife		windward	
whole-heartedly		wig		windy	
wholesale		wild		wine	
wholesome		wilder		wineglass	
wholly		wilderness		wing	
whom		wildest		wink	
whoop		wildly		winner	
whose		wilful		winsome	
whosoever		wilfully		winsomely	
why		wilfulness		winter	
wick		*will*		wintry	
wicked		willingly *or*		wipe	
wickerwork		willingness *or*		wiper	
wicket		willow		wire	

212

wiry		withstood		woo	
wisdom		witless		wood	
wise		witness		wooden	
wisely		witticism		woodland	
wiser		wittily		woodwork	
wisest		wittingly		wool	
wish		witty		woollen woolen	
wishful		wives		woolly	
wistful		wizard		word	
wistfully		wizened		wore	
wit		wobble		work	
witch		woke		worker	
with		wolf		workman	
withal		woman		workmanship	
withdraw		womanhood		workshop	
withdrawal		womanly		world	
withdrawn		women		worldly	
withdrew		won		worldwide	
wither		wonder		worm	
withheld		*wonderful*		worn	
withhold		*wonderfully*		worry	
within		wonderingly		worse	
without		wondrous		worship	
withstand		won't		worst	

213

worsted

worth

worthier

worthiest

worthily

worthless

worthwhile

worthy

would

wound, *n*

wound, *v*

wove

woven

wrangle

wrap

wrapper

wrath

wrathful

wreak

wreath

wreathe

wreck

wreckage

wrench

wrestle

wretch

wretched

wretchedness

wriggle

wrily

wring

wringer

wrinkle

wrist

wristlet

wristwatch

writ

write

write-off

writer

write-up

writhe

written

wrong

wrongdoer

wrong*doing*

wrongful

wrongfully

wrongly

wrote

wrought

wrung

wry

wyvern

214

X

xenophobia	X-ray	xylophone
xerox	xylonite	xylophonist

Y

yacht	yes	young
yank	yesman	younger
yap	yesterday	youngest
yard	yet	youngster
yarn	yew	your
year	yield	yours
yearbook	yodel	yourself
yearly	yoga	yourselves
yearn	yoke	youth
yeast	yokel	youthful
yell	yolk	youthfulness
yellow	yonder	yuletide
yelp	you	yo-yo

Z

zeal		zero		zodiac		
zealot		zest		zone		
zealous		zigzag		zoological		
zealously		zinc		zoologist		
zebra		zipper		zoology		
zenith		zircon		zoom		
zephyr		zither		zoonomy		

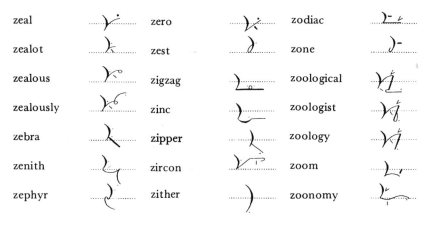

216

List of Proper Names

Abraham		Bertha		Daniel			
Adams		Betty		David			
Agnes		Brenda		Davis			
Aileen		Brian		Den(n)is			
Albert		Bruce		Derek			
Al(l)an		Bryant		Diana			
Alexander		Buchanan		Donald			
Andrew		Campbell		Dorothy			
Angela		Carol		Edward			
Ann(e)		Caroline		Edwin			
Ant(h)ony		Catherine		Eileen			
Armstrong		Charles		Eleanor			
Arnold		Christopher		Elizabeth			
Arthur		Clara		Emerson			
Barbara		Clarence		Eric			
Beatrice		Clark		Ernest			
Benjamin		Cynthia		Ethel			

217

Fillmore		Jacqueline		Louis	
Frances		James		Louise	
Francis		Jane		Luther	
Frank		Janet		Lynne	
Fraser		Jean		Mackenzie	
Frederick		Jennifer		Malcolm	
Geoffrey		Jeremy		Margaret	
George		Jessie (Jesse)		Margery	
Gerald		Jill		Marilyn	
Gertrude		John		Marion	
Gillian		Johnson		Marjorie	
Gordon		Jonathan		Marshall	
Harold		Joseph		Martin	
Harriet		Julia		Maureen	
Hazel		Katherine		Maurice	
Helen		Kathleen		Michael	
Henry		Kenneth		Moira	
Herbert		Lawrence		Moore	
Howard		Leonard		Morris	
Hugh		Lesley		Nancy	
Ia(i)n		Leslie		Napolean	
Irving		Lewis		Neil	
Isaac		Lillian		Nelson	
Isabel		Linda		Nic(h)olas	

218

Nigel	Raymond	Shakespeare
Norman	Richard	Sharon
Oliver	Richardson	Sheila
Olivia	Robert	Sidney
Owen	Roger	Simon
Patricia	Ro(w)land	Smith
Patrick	Rosamund	Stephanie
Paul	Roy	Stephen (Steven)
Pauline	Rupert	Stewart (Stuart)
Peggy	Russell	Susan
Peter	Ruth	T(h)eresa
Philip	Samuel	Thomas
Phyllis	Sarah	Tracey
Rachel	Seamus	William
Ralph	Sean	Wilson

List of World Place Names

Abyssinia

Adelaide

Aden

Afghanistan

Africa

Ajax

Akron

Alabama

Alaska

Albania

Albany

Alberta

Albuquerque

Alexander

Alexandria

Alfred

Algeria

Algonquin

Allegheny

Allentown

Altoona

America

Amherst

Amman

Amsterdam

Angola

Annapolis

Antigua

Arabia

Arctic

Argentina

Arizona

Arkansas

Armenia

Asia

Athabasca

Athens

Atlanta

Atlantic

Atlantic City

Augusta

Aurora

Austin

Australia

Austria

Bahamas

Baghdad

Baltic

Baltimore

Banff

Bangkok

Bangladesh

Barbados

Barcelona

Barrie

Bathurst

Baton Rouge

Bavaria

Bayonne

Bedford

Beirut

Belfast

Belgium

Belgrade

Belleville

Berkeley

Berlin

Bermuda

Berne

Bethlehem

Binghamton

Birmingham

Bismarck

Boise

Bolivia

Bombay

Bonn

Borneo

Boston

Boulder

Brampton

Brandon

Brantford

Brasilia

Brazil

Brazilian

Bremen

Bridgeport

Brisbane

Britain

British
Columbia

Briton

Brittany

Broadway

Brockville

Bronx

Brooklyn

Brunei

Brussels

Bryant

Bucharest

Budapest

Buffalo

Buenos Aires

Bulgaria

Bunker Hill

Burgundy

Burlington

Burma

Butte

Cairo

Calcutta

Calgary

California

Cambodia

Cambridge

Camden

Campbellton

Canberra

Canada

Canadian

221

Canton	Cologne	Danzig
Capetown	Colombia	Dar es Salaam
Capitol	Colombian	Dartmouth
Caracas	Colorado	Davenport
Caribbean	Columbus	Darwin
Carolina	Concord	Dayton
Carson City	Connecticut	Dawson Creek
Casablanca	Coolidge	Delaware
Catskill	Cornell	Delhi (India)
Cedar Rapids	Corner Brook	Delhi (N.A.)
Charlotte	Cornwall	Denmark
Charlottetown	Corsica	Denver
Chatam	Costa Rica	Des Moines
Chattanooga	Covington	Detroit
Chautauqua	Cranbrook	Dominica
Cheyenne	Cuba	Dorchester
Chicago	Crete	Dover
Chile	Cypriot	Dresden
Chilean	Cyprus	Dublin
China	Czecho-slovakia	Duluth
Chinese		Dundas
Cincinnati	Dallas	Durban
Cleveland	Damascus	Durham
Cobourg	Danish	Dutch

222

East Indies

East Kildonan

Ecuador

Edgar

Edinburgh

Edmonton

Edmundston

Egypt

Egyptian

El Paso

England

English

Erie

Ethiopia

Euphrates

Europe

European

Evanston

Evansville

Everest

Fall River

Fargo

Fiji

Finland

Flin Flon

Flint

Florence

Florida

Formosa

Fort Erie

Fort Wayne

Fort Worth

France

Frankfort

Fredericton

French

Fresno

Fulton

Galt

Galveston

Garfield

Gary

Gaspe

Geneva

Genoa

Georgetown

Georgia

Geraldton

German

Germany

Glace Bay

Glasgow

Grande Prairie

Grand Rapids

Great Britain

Great Falls

Greece

Greek

Greenland

Greenwich

Grimsby

Guatemala

Guam

Guelph

Hague

Haiti

Halifax

Hanoi

Hamburg

223

Hamilton	Huronia	Japanese
Harding		Jeferson City
Harlem	Iceland	Jersey City
Harrisburg	Idaho	Johannes-burg
Harrison	Illinois	Jerusalem
Hartford	India	Johnstown
Harvard	Indiana	Jordan
Havana	Indianapolis	Juneau
Hawaii	Indonesia	
Hayes	Iowa	Kamloops
Helena	Iran	Kansas
Helsinki	Ireland	Kansas City
Holland	Irish	Kapuskasing
Hollywood	Islington	Kashmir
Honduras	Israel	Kelowna
Hong Kong	Istanbul	Kenora
Honolulu	Italian	Kentucky
Hoover	Italy	Kenya
Houston	Iraq	Kiev
Hudson		Kingston
Hugh	Jackson	Kitchener
Hull	Jacksonville	Knoxville
Hungary	Jamaica	Kobe
Huntington	Japan	Korea

Kuwait

Labrador

Lafayette

Lagos

Lake Superior

Lansing

Laos

La Salle

Laval

Leamington

Lebanon

Leeds

Leipzig

Leningrad

Lethbridge

Lexington

Liberia

Libya

Lima

Lincoln

Lindsay

Lisbon

Little Rock

Liverpool

London

Long Beach

Long Island

Longueuil

Los Angeles

Louisiana

Louisville

Lowell

Lusaka

Luxembourg

Macon

Madagascar

Madeira

Madison

Madras

Madrid

Maine

Malaya

Malta

Manchester

Manchuria

Manhattan

Manila

Manitoba

Markham

Marseilles

Maryland

Massachusetts

McKeesport

McKinley

Medicine Hat

Mediterranean

Melbourne

Memphis

Mexico

Mexico City

Miami

Michigan

Midland

Milan

Milwaukee

Minneapolis

Minnesota

Miquelon

Mississauga

Mississippi

225

Missouri
Mobile
Mohawk
Monaco
Moncton
Mongolia
Monroe
Monrovia
Montana
Montevideo
Montgomery
Montpelier
Montserrat ... or ...
Montreal
Moore
Moose Jaw
Morocco
Moscow
Mount Vernon
Munich

Nairobi
Nanaimo
Nanking
Naples
Nashville
Nassau
Natal
Nebraska
Nelson
Nepal
Netherlands
Nevada
New Bedford
New Brunswick
New Delhi
New Glasgow
New Guinea
New Hampshire
New Haven
New Jersey
New Mexico
New Orleans
New Rochelle
New Westminister
New York
New York City
New York State
New Zealand
Newmarket
Newark
Newfoundland
Newport
Niagara
Niagara Falls
Niagara-on-the-Lake
Nicaragua
Niger
Nigeria
Nile
Norfolk
Normandy
North America
North Battleford
North Bay
North Carolina
North Dakota
North Vancouver
Northern Ireland
Northwest Territories
Norway
Norwegian

Nova Scotia	Pakistan	Poland
	Palermo	Polish
Oakland	Palestine	Polk
Oakville	Panama	Pontiac
Ohio	Paraguay	Portage la Prairie
Oklahoma	Paris	Port Alberni
Olympic	Pasadena	Port Colborne
Olympia	Passaic	Port Coquitlam
Omaha	Paterson	Port Moody
Oman	Peace River	Portland
Ontario	Peking	Portsmouth
Oregon	Pembroke	Portugal
Orient	Pennsylvania	Potomac
Orillia	Penticton	Prague
Orlando	Peoria	Preston
Oromocto	Perth	Prince Albert
Osaka	Peru	Prince Edward Island
Oslo	Peterborough	
Oshawa	Philadelphia	Prince George
Ottawa	Phillippines	Prince Rupert
Owen Sound	Phoenix	Providence
Oxford	Pierre	Puerto Rico
	Pittsburg	
Pacific	Plymouth	Quebec

227

Queensland	Sacramento	San Francisco
Queenstown	Saigon	San Jose
	Saint John	San Juan
Rabat	St. Albert	Santa Fe
Racine	St. Boniface	Santiago
Raleigh	St. Catherines	Sardinia
Reading	St. James Assiniboia	Sarnia
Red Deer	St. John's	Saskatchewan
Red River	St. Lawrence	Saskatoon
Regina	St. Louis	Saudi Arabia
Reno	St. Lucia	Sault Ste. Marie
Rhine	St. Paul	Savannah
Rhode Island	St. Petersburg	Schenectady
Rhodesia	St. Pierre	Scotch
Richmond	St. Thomas	Scotland
Richmond Hill	St. Vincent	Scottish
Rio de Janeiro	St. Vital	Scranton
Rochester	Salem	Seattle
Rocky Mountains	Salisbury	Selkirk
Rome	Salt Lake City	Senegal
Roosevelt	Salvador	Seoul
Rotterdam	Samoa	Shanghai
Romania	San Antonio	Sheffield
Russia	San Diego	Sherbrooke

228

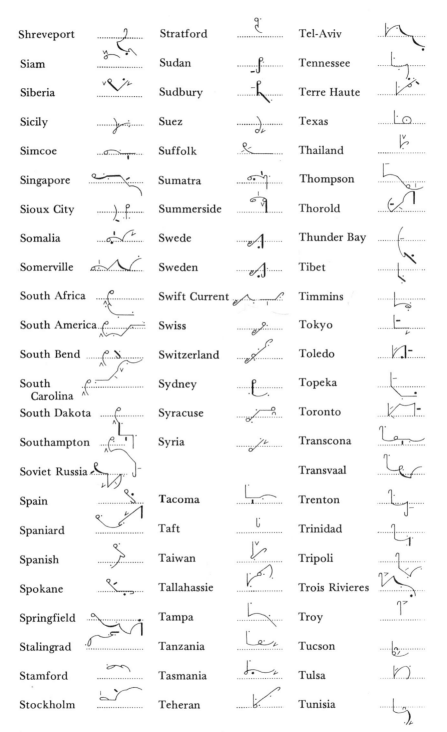

Shreveport	Stratford	Tel-Aviv
Siam	Sudan	Tennessee
Siberia	Sudbury	Terre Haute
Sicily	Suez	Texas
Simcoe	Suffolk	Thailand
Singapore	Sumatra	Thompson
Sioux City	Summerside	Thorold
Somalia	Swede	Thunder Bay
Somerville	Sweden	Tibet
South Africa	Swift Current	Timmins
South America	Swiss	Tokyo
South Bend	Switzerland	Toledo
South Carolina	Sydney	Topeka
South Dakota	Syracuse	Toronto
Southampton	Syria	Transcona
Soviet Russia		Transvaal
Spain	Tacoma	Trenton
Spaniard	Taft	Trinidad
Spanish	Taiwan	Tripoli
Spokane	Tallahassie	Trois Rivieres
Springfield	Tampa	Troy
Stalingrad	Tanzania	Tucson
Stamford	Tasmania	Tulsa
Stockholm	Teheran	Tunisia

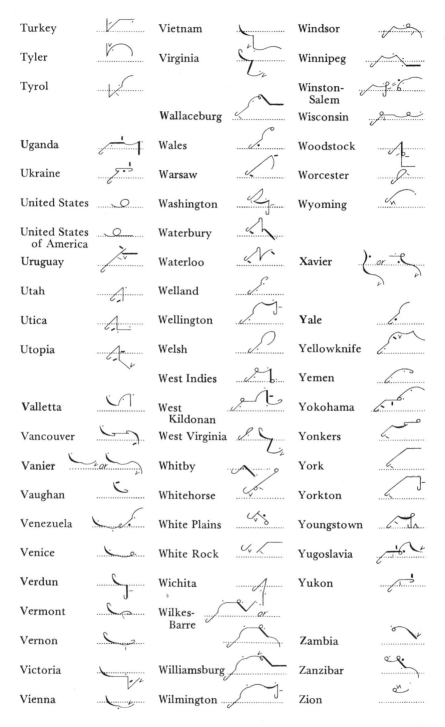

Turkey		Vietnam		Windsor	
Tyler		Virginia		Winnipeg	
Tyrol				Winston-Salem	
		Wallaceburg		Wisconsin	
Uganda		Wales		Woodstock	
Ukraine		Warsaw		Worcester	
United States		Washington		Wyoming	
United States of America		Waterbury			
Uruguay		Waterloo		Xavier	
Utah		Welland			
Utica		Wellington		Yale	
Utopia		Welsh		Yellowknife	
		West Indies		Yemen	
Valletta		West Kildonan		Yokohama	
Vancouver		West Virginia		Yonkers	
Vanier		Whitby		York	
Vaughan		Whitehorse		Yorkton	
Venezuela		White Plains		Youngstown	
Venice		White Rock		Yugoslavia	
Verdun		Wichita		Yukon	
Vermont		Wilkes-Barre			
Vernon				Zambia	
Victoria		Williamsburg		Zanzibar	
Vienna		Wilmington		Zion	

Some Common SI Units

Angstrom		kiloohm	
ampere		kilopascal	
candela		kilosecond	
centimetre		kilovolt	
coulomb		kilowatt	
cubic metre		kilowatt hour	
degree Celcius		litre	
farad		megahertz	
gram		megajoule	
hectare		megaohm	
henry		megavolt	
joule		metre	
kelvin		metre per second	
kilogram		microampere	
kilohertz		micrometre	
kilojoule		microsecond	
kilometre		milliampere	

milligram		ohm	
millimetre		pascal	
milliohm		picometre	
millisecond		square metre	
millivolt		tesla	
mole		volt	
nanometre		watt	
newton		weber	

List of Pitman Pacers

a/an	dear	how	
able to	do	I/eye	
accord/according/ according to	dollar/had	immediate	
all	enlarge	immediately	
almost	enlarged	in/any	
also	enlargement	influence	
altogether	eye/I	influenced	
always	for	influential	
and	gentleman	information	
any/in	gentlemen	is/his	
anything	had/dollar	it	
are	has/as	January	
as/has	have	large	
be	he	largely	
before	his/is	larger	
but	hour/our	largest	
cannot	hours	manufacture	

manufactured	satisfactory		too	
manufacturing	several		two	
manufacturer	shall		United States	
manufactures	should		United States of America	
more	something		very	
nevertheless	thank		we	
New York	that		which	
nothing	the		who	
notwithstanding	their		will	
of	there		without	
oh/owe	therefore		wonderful/ly	
on	thing		would	
our/hour	think		year	
ours	this		yesterday	
owe/oh	this is		you	
owing	to/too/two		your	
put	today		yours	
responsible	to be		yourself	
responsibility	together		yours sincerely	

NORTHWEST COMMUNITY COLLEGE